Who Are You?
What Do You Want?

4

Questions That
Will Change Your Life

Mick Ukleja, PhD, and Robert L. Lorber, PhD

A PERIGEE BOOK

A PERIGEE BOOK
Published by the Penguin Group
Penguin Group (USA) Inc.
375 Hudson Street, New York, New York 10014, USA
Penguin Group (Canada), 90 Eglinton Avenue East, Suite 700, Toronto, Ontario M4P 2Y3, Canada
(a division of Pearson Penguin Canada Inc.)
Penguin Books Ltd., 80 Strand, London WC2R 0RL, England
Penguin Group Ireland, 25 St. Stephen's Green, Dublin 2, Ireland (a division of Penguin Books Ltd.)
Penguin Group (Australia), 250 Camberwell Road, Camberwell, Victoria 3124, Australia
(a division of Pearson Australia Group Pty. Ltd.)
Penguin Books India Pvt. Ltd., 11 Community Centre, Panchsheel Park, New Delhi—110 017, India
Penguin Group (NZ), 67 Apollo Drive, Rosedale, North Shore 0632, New Zealand
(a division of Pearson New Zealand Ltd.)
Penguin Books (South Africa) (Pty.) Ltd., 24 Sturdee Avenue, Rosebank, Johannesburg 2196,
South Africa

Penguin Books Ltd., Registered Offices: 80 Strand, London WC2R 0RL, England

While the author has made every effort to provide accurate telephone numbers and Internet addresses at the time of publication, neither the publisher nor the author assumes any responsibility for errors, or for changes that occur after publication. Further, the publisher does not have any control over and does not assume any responsibility for author or third-party websites or their content.

First Perigee edition: September 2009
Adapted from *Who Are You and What Do You Want?*, published by Meredith Books in 2008.

Library of Congress Cataloging-in-Publication Data

Ukleja, Mick.
    Who are you? What do you want? : four questions that will change your life / Mick Ukleja and Robert L. Lorber.— 1st Perigee ed.
        p. cm.
    "A Perigee book."
    Includes bibliographical references.
    ISBN 978-0-399-53543-7
    1. Success.   I. Lorber, Robert.   II. Title.
    BV4511.U44 2009
    646.7—dc22   2009016796

PRINTED IN THE UNITED STATES OF AMERICA

10   9   8   7   6   5   4   3   2   1

Most Perigee books are available at special quantity discounts for bulk purchases for sales promotions, premiums, fund-raising, or educational use. Special books, or book excerpts, can also be created to fit specific needs. For details, write: Special Markets, Penguin Group (USA) Inc., 375 Hudson Street, New York, New York 10014.

Who Are You?
What Do You Want?

CONTENTS

'm excited about writing the foreword to *Who Are You? What Do You Want?* for two reasons.

First, I'm a big fan of Mick Ukleja and Bob Lorber. I've known Mick for 10 years. He was a prominent pastor in Orange County for many years, and now he's using his wisdom and skills in other areas. He cofounded the Ukleja Center for Ethical Leadership at California State University, Long Beach, to which he invites leaders such as John Wooden, Patrick Lencioni, me, and others to share their points of view with students. I've known Bob for more than 30 years. He coauthored *Putting the One Minute Manager to Work* with me, is on the board of directors for the Ken Blanchard Companies, and is one of the top management team-building consultants in the world.

The second reason I'm excited about this book is because I believe that effective leadership is really a transformational journey that includes self-leadership, one-on-one leadership, team leadership, and organizational leadership. Self-leadership comes first, because effective leadership starts on the inside. Before you can hope to lead anyone else, you have to know yourself and what you need to be successful. Only when you have experience in leading yourself are you ready to lead others. The key to one-on-one leadership is being able to develop a trusting relationship with others. If you don't know who you are, or what your strengths and weaknesses are, and you are not willing to be vulnerable, you'll never develop a trusting relationship. The same principle applies to team and organizational leadership.

One of the primary mistakes organizations make today is that they spend most of their time and energy trying to solve problems at an organizational level with leaders who haven't asked themselves the fundamental question, "Who am I and what do I want?"

This book is about authentic self-leadership and being true to yourself. Why is the question "Who am I?" so difficult to answer? Perhaps because people don't take the time to reflect on their lives— they're too busy just doing, doing, doing. We have to remember that we're not human doings, we are human beings. This book will help you reflect on your life so that you have a clearer picture of who you are and what you want. This knowledge will become a firm foundation for all your life decisions and choices.

Mick and Bob ask the question "What do you want?" rather than "What do you need?" Doing what you need takes effort and struggle and isn't very motivating. Take the same need and turn it into a want—now that's motivating and far less effort. In the end, more of us prefer to do what we *want* to do rather than what we *need* to do.

I think you're going to enjoy the journey on which Mick and Bob will take you in the pages that follow. You'll start by discovering who you are, then move on to finding out where you are and why you're there. Then you'll explore what you'll do and how you'll do it. Finally, you'll find out who your allies are and how they can help you. These four questions provide you a means to gain perspective and clarity and will help you deal successfully with every personal and professional challenge you may face.

The whole book comes together powerfully at the end when

Bob and Mick present the design for a weekend retreat that you can do by yourself, or with friends or business associates. When you answer the questions in a thoughtful way, you'll come out a better person, because you will know who you are, what you're doing, and what's going to guide your journey.

—Ken Blanchard, coauthor of
The One Minute Manager and *Leading at a Higher Level*

Who Are You?
What Do You Want?

The Choices Are Yours

On the journey to success and happiness in life, it's easy to become frustrated at the inevitable crossroads and detours. Some people give up before they get started; others become discouraged when the journey becomes difficult; still others grow excited by the challenges. And, like the man who was overheard at his school reunion saying, "If I had known those years would be the best years of my life, I would have had more fun!" Some people pass by opportunities that come their way because they don't see the inherent possibilities. Many women and men have seemingly enviable careers and relationships yet wish they were somewhere else doing something else with someone else.

Is life that complicated?

Well, yes and no. There are certainly many complex issues that we all face in a lifetime, but the simple fact is that you can make the choices to take you where you want to be. No one can predict the future, but no one can deny the importance of the choices we make today in how things will play out tomorrow.

When the circumstances of our lives become difficult, the options we have seem to shrink more, or even disappear. Whether you are working as a member of an organization or acting as an individual, a sudden crisis can cause you to become reactionary. It is easy to become immobilized during tough times rather than proactively take charge. People can feel "stuck," which we define as *a regression of the imagination*. In that frame of mind you not only lose your sense of adventure about your life, but you can also feel that things will always remain the same as they now are—in what we call *imagination gridlock*—which causes you to feel as though you have no control whatsoever. The concepts in this book will show you how much control you really have. Getting unstuck allows you to make the most of life, even when something *happens to you*. You will never waste another crisis doing anything less than what's productive for you or your organization. Getting unstuck is a very freeing and empowering process.

Over the past 30 years, working both individually and together, we've had the privilege of mentoring, counseling, and consulting thousands of entrepreneurs, employees, teams, managers, executives, and CEOs across corporate America. The priceless insights of our family members, friends, students, and colleagues have informed our quest to discover the traits that happy and successful people share in their personal and family lives as well as at work. And we've come to understand that life isn't so easily segmented—if you don't feel great at work, you won't at home either, and vice versa. As one 34-year-old executive said to us, "I'm getting a B at work and a C-minus at home. I refuse to think I'm becoming mediocre. Is it the job, or is it me?"

More Than Mediocre

No one we know has ever had a goal to be mediocre, yet that's what happens when people compromise themselves in a world driven by hyperkinetic activity where they feel like they have to compartmentalize their work, home, personal, and spiritual lives, like actors on a rotating stage in the play *Stop the World—I Want to Get Off.* What we all desperately need is a way to step off the stage, take a seat in the balcony, and look at the big picture, the whole stage, the scenery, the plot. Or to change metaphors, we need to kick the cord out of the treadmill.

From the work that we've done with countless individuals and groups and the observations we've made, we have developed a way to uncover one's uniqueness by asking four simple questions that provide a model for self-reflection and life planning. Each of these questions provides a distinct facet or dimension through which you can examine your life.

This four-dimensional process is not about complicating your life with new ideas; rather it's about discovering what's already within you. Learning from other people is certainly important; learning about yourself, from yourself, is even more important. These Four Questions are your first steps to self-discovery.

Four Questions That Will Change Your Life

"Who are you and what do you want?"

"Where are you and why are you there?"

"What will you do and how will you do it?"

"Who are your allies and how can they help?"

Over the years, we have presented these Four Questions in this life-planning process with thousands of people at every stage of life. When we talk to high school students, they tell us that no one has ever asked them these questions before. Usually, astute teenagers tell us, when they are asked what they want to do in life, the questioner is really looking for the "right" answer, ready to tell them what they "should" do.

When we lead classes with MBA students, the questions they ask us are not about business skills or leadership strategies; they are primarily life-planning questions. On the verge of launching their professional careers with nothing to hold them back from going anywhere they want, they are asking, "How can I know what I will ultimately enjoy? How can I find more than just a job? I think I know what I want to do, but how will I get there?"

Working professionals often confess that they don't have many choices left. They fear they are running out of time to make career changes. Yet they feel stuck in what they are doing. One successful dentist told us, "I really hate being a dentist, but I'm making two hundred thousand dollars a year, and I don't know what else I can do. If I quit, what would I do?"

A Compass to Guide You

The Four Questions can become a reliable, easy-to-use compass to guide you. But it doesn't mean that the journey will be easy. Although many successful people with whom we've worked may make it look effortless, the journey for the best of your life requires focus, determination, discipline—and thinking and behaving four-dimensionally with these questions as your compass points.

Although self-awareness and achieving your goals are important, we are convinced that the experiences you have and the relationships that you build, in both your personal and professional lives, are what really make life worth living. The Four Questions will help you explore all of these facets of your life.

Enjoy your own journey and the best of your life!

—Mick Ukleja and Bob Lorber

ONE

Your Journey Begins with a Destination

"Would you tell me, please, which way I ought to go from here?"

"That depends a good deal on where you want to get to," said the Cat.

"I don't much care where—" said Alice.

"Then it doesn't matter which way you go," said the Cat.

"—so long as I get somewhere," Alice added as an explanation.

"Oh, you're sure to do that," said the Cat, "if you only walk long enough."

—from Lewis Carroll's *Alice's Adventures in Wonderland*

Matt, a 65-year-old executive vice president of a Fortune 500 company, expressed it as well as anyone: "I went to good schools, got married, landed a job with a great company, and was promoted through the ranks. As a result, the lifestyle that my family enjoyed has been pretty wonderful by all accounts, but now that I'm about to retire, it feels as though everything I've done has been wrapped around my work. I'm about to leave and the new guy will come in and put down some new wall-to-wall in my office and it will be like I never existed. The 'A' tables at the events and restaurants will disappear. And I'll be just another guy waiting for a tee time at the golf club.

"Who am I?

"Suddenly, without the job, the perks, or the first-class trips to Paris, London, Singapore, and Beijing, I'm left feeling naked, stripped of my title and even a business card. I've been telling every-one that I wanted to play more golf, but not all day, every day.

"Now when I look back, it's as though I spent my life living it for others—*reacting* to obligations at home and on the job. Maybe this sounds self-serving. But if you ask most of the people who know me, they'd probably say that I had lived a charmed life.

"Nevertheless, I'm feeling kind of numb and empty—and I would never have admitted that to anyone. I am unprepared for the next phase of my life. I had terrific strategic plans for my company, but I never took the time to create a life plan for myself.

"Realistically, I have maybe 10—at the most, 15—vital years left. So when I ask myself the question 'Who am I and what do I want?' honestly, I don't have a clue. I never really thought about it before. My identity has been tied to what I was, not who I am or will be."

Anna, 44, a former senior editor at a women's magazine, was one vic-tim of many in a massive layoff. A single mom with two school-aged girls, she sits in her kitchen staring at her severance check, trying to figure out a way to pay the rent, buy groceries, and cover her kids' tuitions, among other obligations in the next few months. When she sees that her six-year-old daughter is walking funny because the hand-me-down shoes she's wearing are too small, it's the proverbial straw that broke the camel's back and she breaks down in tears. "Figuring out who I am," she says, "seems like a luxury I can't afford right now. Frankly, I feel overwhelmed and uncertain about where to turn next."

"If you don't know where you are going, you might end up someplace else." —Yogi Berra

---

Many people feel that their lives should be different from what they're living right now. They have a yearning for something more. Young people in finance or technology jobs are working 70 hours a week with salaries into six figures, yet when asked, they don't seem to know what they want and don't see how they can stop long enough to find out. Middle-aged men and women think about what they have had to give up to make a living to support their families; struggling simply to keep their heads above water consumes their time and energy. Mothers who left the workplace to raise a family believe that their skills are outmoded and that they are unqualified to get a decent job anymore. And people in all professions, like Anna, who thought their jobs were secure are rudely awakened from their complacency when the pink slips land on their desks. What is Plan B?

Busy entrepreneurs who once thought they were pretty clear about what they wanted out of their lives and jobs say they feel trapped by the endless decisions they face, no matter whether they're at work or at home. And when they finally seem to have the financial wherewithal to do what they want, they think their businesses would suffer if they took time off to focus on other parts of their lives. Many successful executives, like Matt, confess they don't know what they will do when they retire because their self-image has been completely defined by their corporate titles.

None of these people have given themselves the time to reflect. They find the exercise uncomfortable or intimidating or think it will be simply a waste of their time. Yet most go on with the hope that in the midst of this chaos in their lives, they'll stumble across something better.

Reality Check

Do some people avoid going for a medical checkup because they're afraid of finding out their health condition is serious, or because they instinctively feel they will need to alter their lifestyle to be healthy? Similar fears keep many people from asking the seemingly simple questions: "Who am I?" and "What do I want?" Their responses, when they come, are often vague and uncertain, changing from day to day. Is it because they don't know? Or is it because they fear what the answers will be? Answering the questions "Who am I?" and "What do I want?" forces you to get right to the point: What is the point of my life? What is my purpose? Some men and women tell us they already know who they are and what they want, yet when we probe a little deeper for specifics they admit, "OK, I am stumped."

Setting a Course

When the great explorers like Magellan, Columbus, and Vespucci sailed to new worlds, either they had no maps or the maps they did have were dangerously unreliable. They used the North Star to navigate because it was the one constant they could rely on. Likewise there are no maps for you to follow on the journey of your life. But you do have a North Star by which to navigate: your North Star is being true to yourself.

Being truthful with yourself becomes your navigational tool to stay on course. The truth is your internal compass, automatically pointing you in the right direction. A commitment to the truth about yourself always serves you well, even in uncharted waters with unexpected weather.

Through all the challenges, changes, and transitions in life, one thing should be standard operating procedure: be true to yourself. When truth is your personal ally, three things happen:

First, you feel better about yourself. You travel light, without the baggage of phoniness or a hidden past. Second, you have less stress and conflict in your life; you don't have the fallout that eventually catches up to people who lie to themselves and others. Third, you have integrity and are respected by the people who count. You are part of many communities—work, family, neighborhood, and more.

Get Out of Your Own Way

What gets in the way of knowing who you are and what you want? The short answer is: you do. You get in your way. But when you have clarity about your destination, you lead yourself. You do not allow other people's agendas, events, or situations to lead you. As leadership expert Warren Bennis says, "You become authentic. The word 'authentic' has as its root the word 'author.' You become the author of your life rather than a copy or shadow of someone else's. Authenticity is doing what you say is important to you."

The road is not always easy, yet when you know who you are, what you want tends to show up.

Making Course Corrections

As any pilot will tell you, if you take off from Los Angeles and want to land at New York's JFK Airport, yet are off only one compass degree to the north, you'll end up somewhere in White Plains, New York, about 26 miles away. Just one degree—that's 0.2 percent—and you will have committed what the FAA calls a "gross navigational error." Stray off course only five degrees—barely 1 percent—and you arrive in Albany, 126 miles from New York City. A seemingly small decision becomes a larger issue as you travel farther and farther.

Mark was a successful entrepreneur who had it made—great wife, wonderful kids, beautiful home, good health, and a successful career. It certainly seemed that his life was on course.

"I was working really hard building my business and had everything cranked up to light speed. Then one day I got a letter delivered to my desk. I looked at the return address and noticed something rather odd—it was from my wife.

"The letter began: 'Dear Mark, I'm writing this letter because it's difficult to get your attention these days' and went on to describe some of the important parts of our life that I was ignoring because of my concentration on my business. 'The pressures of career and a growing family,' she continued, 'can camouflage an eroding marriage relationship.'

"Eroding marriage! Ouch. She had my attention."

At some point Mark lost his way and didn't realize it. But he knew he needed a course correction. "At first I felt helpless—I was so focused on what I was doing with my business that I'd ignored many important things. I had made my job the priority over my connections with my wife, the kids, our parents and siblings, and friends.

"That day, I canceled my lunch date, grabbed a notebook, and headed to a nearby park. I knew that I had to try to make sense of things in the best way I knew how—write it down. And it was as if my pen exploded onto the page. I was, as it turns out, unconsciously asking myself 'Who am I?' and 'What do I want?' I could barely write fast enough to keep up with my mind as my dreams and goals spilled out onto the page:

> "Begin today to show Laura how important she is to me.

> "Spend more intimate and uninterruptible time with my family and good friends.

> "Make more personal connections with people—especially those closest to me.

> "It is up to me to make my life work.

"After about a half hour of this, the sense of panic subsided. Having that handwritten list right in front of me made me realize how far I had drifted away from my values. It became clear to me what the real course of my life should be, as opposed to the one I was following.

"Coming to terms with the truth was painful, but was extremely enlightening and powerful once I allowed myself to be guided by it. I was willing to make any course corrections to keep Laura and regain the life we had planned together. Too much was at stake not to pay attention. That afternoon my wonderful, loving wife received two dozen yellow roses and a message from me that said, 'Thank you, Laura. I needed that!'"

For Mark, the wake-up call from his wife was what he needed to start him thinking. The short time that he took for reflection provided his course correction. However, writing down his goals didn't minimize his need for action. As management expert and coauthor Henry Mintzberg wrote in the *Harvard Business Review*,

"Action without reflection is thoughtless. Reflection without action is passive."[1]

For Mark, like many, the problem was not a lack of destination but rather a vague notion of happiness and success. He'd wandered off course and didn't realize he'd lost his way because his destination was nonspecific. And he now had the motivation to change because too much was at stake not to pay attention.

Motivation to Change

Five years from now your business and personal life won't be exactly as it is today. You wouldn't want it to be. Most likely you're probably hoping that your life and lifestyle have improved. Even with the best of intentions, however, people rarely accomplish meaningful change unless they experience a crisis. It's a sense of urgency—real or imagined—that motivates most people to evaluate their lives, make long-overdue changes, or break away from their normal routines.

People often need a crisis point to force them to ask crucial questions in their lives—just as Mark was prompted by the letter from his wife to take the time to ask himself the hard questions. But in reality, no one needs to wait for a crisis. You don't have to experience everything firsthand to learn. You don't have to file bankruptcy to learn a better way of managing business. The tragedy of waiting for a crisis is that you don't see the light until you feel the heat. But when you look for the light, the insight arrives before the heat comes. Prevention and anticipation are the best solution. Have health checkups on a regular basis instead of waiting for symptoms to appear. Pack your parachute before you jump—it's difficult to do on the way down!

So what keeps so many people from making changes? They say they want to change; they know that a change would lead to a better life. What holds them back? In a word, it's tropophobia—the fear of change. The most powerful enemy of change is fear.

We all harbor at least a little fear that change is the death of a part of ourselves. When we think about change, the first thought that hits us at an emotional level is usually not what we are going to gain but what we will have to give up.

Leaving the familiar to the unknown can be momentarily numbing or scary. Some people can have a sudden, unexpected feeling of loss even at the same time they experience a happy event, like the day they get married or start a new job or launch a major project. When you move beyond any initial fear of what you may be giving up to the advantages of what will be—you are free.

What You Have Is Not Who You Are

Many people in Western nations today suffer from unipolar depression—having bad feelings without a specific cause. The incidence of all types of depression today is an epidemic. The World Health Organization (WHO) estimates that 100 million people in the United States, Canada, and the European Union are clinically depressed. In the United States the impact is $83 billion a year in mental health costs and lost productivity.

Mark's experience is not uncommon. Sociological studies show that as income goes up so does the sense of well-being, but only so far. Once we cover the basic needs of food, clothing, and shelter, money and happiness are no longer directly correlated because it appears that goals and benchmarks keep moving. What we want—as opposed to what we need—may never be satisfied, no matter how much we have. The more we have, the more we seem to want.

In *Trading Up: Why Consumers Want New Luxury Goods*, authors Michael J. Silverstein and Neil Fiske report on a survey of consumers that shows a country full of overwhelmed, isolated, lonely, worried, and unhappy Americans.[2] The statistics can be discouraging:

Never have enough time	54.8%
Don't get enough sleep	53.8%
Don't spend enough time with friends	51.5%
Worry about health	40.1%
Working harder than ever	39.0%
Feel a great deal of stress	36.6%
Don't feel appreciated	36.5%
Am happy with personal appearance	30.5%
Am happy in romantic relationships	17.8%

Despite expanding purchasing power and consumer knowledge combined with an almost limitless assortment of goods and services at their disposal, only 39 percent agreed with the statement "I have the right balance in my life"; only 37 percent with the statement "I feel like a part of my community"; and only 35 percent—that's about one in three people—with the statement "I have a lot of close friends." What's going on?

In his book *The Progress Paradox*, Gregg Easterbrook describes Western nations as having "more of everything except happiness." He points to studies that show that a lack of money can lead to unhappiness, but having it does not cause happiness. Millionaires are no happier than people of average income. The young are supposed to be happy and carefree, but for most people happiness increases with age. And curiously, disabled and chronically ill people report a slightly higher sense of well-being than the population at large not because they are more financially secure but because they have a higher appreciation for the value of their own lives.[3]

Fine-Tuning Your Destination

"From the time I was nine years old," Dr. Steve Hadley recalls, "I had a love for helping animals. We always had a lot of animals around when I was growing up, so several experiences helped shape my passion for veterinary medicine. Later, while managing a veterinary emergency referral practice, I learned that I also loved the management side of my work, which led me to enroll in the Executive MBA program at Pepperdine University.

"At the time I had heard Mick Ukleja speaking on the topic of following your dreams and passions. 'Who are you and what do you want?' kept reverberating in my brain.

"I finished my degree program at the Wharton School and went to work in San Francisco for Goldman Sachs. But something wasn't right.

"What was I doing putting on a suit at four a.m. and working on the thirtieth floor of the Bank of America building in downtown San Francisco? How did I get here? Suddenly my life wasn't making any sense to me."

Through the years, Steve and Mick had stayed in touch. "What would your life look like if you weren't stuck?" Mick asked him. "What would your life look like if it made more sense? Where did you lose sight of your destination?"

A short time later Steve had his own insight into the blindingly obvious: "It was Halloween and my oldest son, Nathan, wanted to dress up as a veterinarian. It was the image of him in my blue surgical scrubs with the embroidered 'Dr. Hadley' on the pocket, holding several stuffed animals with bandages on them, that reconnected me with my real passion."

Steve reflected on the sequence of events in his life and realized that he hadn't left the veterinary industry because he didn't like being a veterinarian. He loved management and finances, too, but he hadn't considered how he could bring all these disparate elements together. After some reflection—and considerable research—he resigned from his banking job to join the Veterinary Centers of America, a network of some 175 hospitals. By taking on responsibility for 45 of those centers, he combined his strengths in business management and finance with his love for animals in a purposeful and meaningful way.

If you know who you are, then what you want tends to show up.

You can land exactly where you want professionally and personally by charting the course of your work and life. The two can never be neatly and cleanly divided because each is an integral part of the other. In the journey to your destination, the weight of your cargo is an important factor in taking off and landing. How heavy is your emotional baggage? Do you have enough stamina or discipline to complete the trip? Are you fueled with your own set of values? Is your personal integrity stowed securely aboard? How will you be nourished during your journey—physically, emotionally, mentally, and spiritually? Who is your trusted copilot? Does your crew have the same destination? If they don't want to go where you're going, what will be compromised? What is your estimated time of arrival? Making stops along the way means it will take longer to get to your destination. Is there a faster way? What will you do after you get there? The truth about who you are and what you want is your guide, making the journey to your destination safe and enjoyable for you and your crew.

For Reflection
Personal Destination Setting and Planning

The more you know about yourself, the more you will learn from yourself and your experiences. Now that you've started thinking about your destination in terms of your work, family, and self, here are some questions for further reflection. Your answers will help you prepare for your *Who Am I and What Do I Want?* Personal Retreat, which is outlined in the final chapter of this book.

> If I received a special-delivery letter from someone at work, a family member, or a friend reminding me of something important in my life that I was forgetting, what would that letter say?

> If I could make a change and be assured of succeeding, how would my life be different from the life I am living right now?

> During the past year, which work-related activities did I enjoy most? Why? Which family-related activities? Why? Which personal activities? Why?

> When and how do I take the time to reflect on my career and personal life?

> Which action, if I did it immediately, would have the greatest positive effect on my life? My work?

TWO

Discovering Your Truth

All truths are easy to understand once they are discovered; the point is to discover them.

—Galileo Galilei

Frances Hesselbein, chairman of the Board of Governors of the Leader to Leader Institute and holder of a Presidential Medal of Freedom, recalled a touching experience when she was preparing to speak on challenges of leadership in the 21st century to business, government, and nonprofit leaders in China. Before she went, she had met with Chairman Shao Ming Lo, a business leader who is dedicated to supporting education in many ways. She was concerned about using a particular word in her speeches that might be awkward or embarrassing. "At the end of my speech," she told him, "I would like to say, 'We keep the faith,' by way of referring to our role and obligations as leaders. How does that translate?" Chairman Shao Ming Lo replied, "Oh, please use that, for in Chinese *faith* translates as *truth*."

We must first and foremost be truthful with ourselves in order to have faith in who we are and what we want.

The Truth Is Your North Star

As discussed in the previous chapter, the one constant on which early explorers could rely was the North Star. In your life's journey, your North Star is being true to yourself. Usually when people speak of telling the truth, they mean being truthful with other people. That's highly commendable. But even more important is telling yourself the truth. It's easy to tell yourself something other than the unvarnished truth. Self-deception is, well, deceptive. Do you ever hear yourself saying things like this:

"This one doesn't count."

"I really tried."

"If you only knew . . ."

"I did it for you (or the kids, or the company, or the shareholders, or . . .)."

"I'm not always . . ."

"That's easy for you, but I . . ."

Such phrases are signals you are making excuses or, rather, excusing yourself from the truth.

Lying to yourself is at best counterproductive and at worst destructive. Telling yourself the unvarnished truth is the most liberating action you can take. It's not always easy. When you are honest with yourself, you make a clear connection between the problems you face and the happiness and success you experience. Avoiding the truth is like using the wrong map: you'll never reach your destination because you won't know the reality of where you are or where you're headed.

John Wooden, basketball Hall of Famer and the winningest coach in college ball, achieved his fame without ever losing sight of who he was or what he wanted. Coach Wooden's father taught him "the two sets of three" for living his life. The first set was about being honest with others:

Never lie
Never cheat
Never steal

The second set was about being honest with himself:

No whining
No complaining
No excuses

"Dad's two sets of three were a compass for me to do the right thing and behave in a proper manner," Wooden says.

In addition to following these rules, Wooden carries a copy of a handwritten, seven-item creed that his father gave him when he graduated from grade school in Centerton, Indiana. The item at the top of his list: "Be true to yourself."

Truth and Personal Accountability

Rarely do we humans hold ourselves accountable; often we point the finger of blame elsewhere. It's become endemic in our culture to blame others. We blame the economy, the boss, the business, employees, coworkers, the media, and educational, medical, legal, and governmental institutions for the ruts in which we find ourselves. We blame the fashion industry because we don't like the way we look. We blame the stock and real estate markets for not making us wealthy. We blame our parents, spouse, children, in-laws, or the entire family for our being stuck. All this blaming and avoiding responsibility leads to a negative, frustrated, depressed, litigious, violent, and angry society.

Chuck Boppell is president and CEO of Worldwide Restaurant Concepts (WRC), which owns and operates the Sizzler and Pat & Oscar's restaurant chains and is a franchisee of 85 KFC restaurants in the United States and Australia. "Shortly after I arrived at WRC," Chuck recalls, "we had an event in Milwaukee where a Sizzler franchisee had some procedural failures cutting and handling meat and introduced E. coli into the system. I learned a great deal from that experience. Our strategy was to be honest and to be out in front telling people what was going on and answering questions and taking responsibility for this problem. We invited the press into our kitchens with their cameras. There was a tremendous amount of pressure for us to back off from this approach—our insurance company was threatening to pull their coverage. They told us point-blank, 'You need to just get your name out of the press and hide! Let it blow over!' Instead our team took the opposite tack, saying to ourselves, 'If we're already on the front page, at least get good mention in along with the bad!' What allowed us to recover most of our business so quickly? I believe it was the way we handled it."

How was it that Chuck was able to stay on track through such a difficult situation? According to Chuck, a teacher planted the value of accountability in his life. "One morning, out of the blue, she sat me down and said, 'The problem you're having is that you're not taking responsibility for what's going on around you—it's never your fault!' That shrapnel of wisdom has remained lodged in my brain ever since."

Chuck learned early from his mentor how important it is to take total—not partial—responsibility for where we are in our lives.

Reacting to Symptoms

Underlying problems at work or home are not always easy to address. If you are less than truthful with yourself, you are like a physician who focuses on symptoms alone instead of the fundamental causes of the problem. That can lead to an endless, unproductive, frustrating search for treatments, trying one thing after another, but all the while your patient becomes sicker.

It's not uncommon to become sidetracked or talked into taking a quick and easy fix, just as Chuck Boppell may have been tempted to do with his problems at his restaurants. A quick fix addresses one thing: a symptom. If you address only a symptom, the underlying problem will fester and worsen. The real problem hides beneath the noise, emotions, and distractions. If there's no real purpose to your life and only symptoms are treated, the cause of a problem is never addressed.

"It's Not My Fault" Is Not Self-Leadership

Unlike Chuck Boppell's approach to solving his company's problem, some people find odd comfort in the role of victim when faced with challenges that never seem to get resolved. Nothing is ever their fault. Circumstances are always beyond their control. They distract themselves and others with their ongoing misfortunes. Rather than taking steps to resolve a bad situation, they waste precious time complaining instead of acting, talking instead of doing. They are not listening to the truth, and they are wasting energy that could be used to tackle one problem at a time using accountability as their guiding force.

If ever there was a person with a rightful claim to victimhood, it is Melanie Washington. Melanie lost her mother, sister, husband, and son to violent deaths, all of them killed by repeat offenders. She turned what could have been self-destructive anger and pity into a mission to make sure that young people coming out of prison have somewhere to go and someone to guide them. With the support of her employer, the Boeing Company, through its Executive on Loan program, Melanie founded the organization Mentoring: A Touch from Above (MATFA). MATFA works with the California Youth Authority. In the past 14 years, more than 1,200 young men have participated in the MATFA program. Of the men in the program, only four have gone back to prison, compared to a state average of some 70 percent. The success has grown out of Melanie's tragedy, her unwillingness to allow herself to sink into victimhood, and her drive to take control of her own life even as she has helped so many others take control of theirs. (Read more about Melanie at www.whoareyoubook.com.)

Truth and Leadership

Leadership is the ability to influence others. Self-leadership, then, consists of the thoughts, behaviors, and strategies that help you exert influence over yourself. You create the biggest barriers to your personal success and happiness when you care more about what others think than you care about what you think.

Self-leadership—the ability to lead yourself—requires confidence to act on your values, no matter what the consequences. It requires the willingness to openly express yourself, no matter how foolish you think you may look to others.

Once you lead yourself, you begin to make a positive and lasting difference. It's the ripple effect. Leaders inspire others to extend themselves far beyond any of their preconceived boundaries and limitations. Great leaders make great things happen because they are committed to their dreams and willing to live by their values at any cost. Their commitment to their own values empowers them to change the world around them.

Reactive or Proactive?

If you don't know what you want—when you don't take ownership of your truth—you react to everyone else's desires, schedules, invitations, requests, and agendas. Rather than going in the direction that's best for you and doing what you need to do to make yourself happy, successful, and healthy, you give up control of your days, evenings, weekends, months, years—life.

Look at your daily planner. Your current level of self-leadership is reflected in every appointment. Do your lunch appointments align with your professional goals? Have you scheduled private time to be with your spouse, loved ones, or family? Are there other business or social events or personal activities you want to do or should do? Is there time to enjoy the things you like?

What happens when you relinquish control of something as simple as your calendar? You subsume your personal and professional goals into other people's needs and wants. When you don't exercise power over the direction of your career or life, your emotions are affected and you become stressed, weary, and angry.

Truth and Fear

In Chapter 1 we introduced the concept of tropophobia—the fear of change—that can hold people back from constructive change. When you can't accept the truth about yourself or your situation, this fear manifests itself in something commonly known as *the impostor syndrome*—the fear that you don't deserve something better. Or that you are unqualified. Despite the opinion of others, despite the truth of the situation, you feel like a fraud—like an impostor. That's fear speaking. When the impostor syndrome takes over, it can have unfortunate consequences.

You: The Impostor

Anyone can be hijacked by the impostor syndrome. It's an all-too-familiar story. The more you achieve, the louder an inner voice whispers, sometimes screams, "Impostor! You don't deserve this!" The impostor syndrome affects your ability to internalize past and current successes. No matter the successes or accomplishments, a person can experience feelings of inadequacy. People who feel like impostors fear the responsibility and visibility that come with success. This is accompanied by a fear of failure, a fear of being found out. They say to themselves, "I can give the impression that I am more competent than I really am," or "I'm afraid that others will discover I'm not qualified for this position," or "My coworkers are going to find out I don't really belong here," or "I don't deserve this great position."

Mick once spoke at a retreat outside Philadelphia where he talked about the impostor fear. The group of high achievers comprised PGA champions, NFL stars, a former vice president of the United States, a major sports broadcaster, one of the top estate attorneys in the nation, and other financially and professionally successful people. The discussion of the impostor syndrome hit them at a gut level. All of them—without exception—admitted it had haunted them throughout their careers. Several confessed to hearing an inner voice whisper, "They'd be disappointed if they really knew," "You're only here because of luck or your contacts," or "They're going to discover the phony you are." Yes, they had learned to cope with it. They had learned how to identify it and push it back. They realized it was irrational to think that way. But nonetheless it was something they had to both acknowledge and dismiss on a regular basis.

Here's one truth: you're probably not as smart as you may want people to think you are. Welcome to the human race. But the fundamental truth is that many people spend too much time worrying about how they measure up to ideals they've created in their own minds. They have a fantasy about how they should be or what they think others expect them to be, whether it's being a brilliant CEO or a perfect mother. You can only be true to yourself—and the best of yourself.

Truth Illuminates Your Journey

Human beings are designed to be physically and emotionally adaptable, flexible, and resilient. We handle an enormous number of challenges in our lives and for the most part we survive just fine. But we also need anchors.

When things start to come unglued, we need to have something in our lives that does not change. There are so many things we can't control, but the one thing over which we do have control is the way that we respond to these challenges and changes. Telling the truth to ourselves becomes our greatest ally in living the life we want. It hurts when others lie to us, but it's more destructive when we lie to ourselves. Honesty with ourselves and others is the key to a successful life and the starting point for answering the questions discussed in the rest of this book.

For Reflection

Think about the following questions before you turn to the next chapter. Review your answers on a regular basis and you will see the degree to which you are managing self-leadership and how you are using the truth as your guiding principal.

Are there areas of my life where I am avoiding the truth?

Have I made excuses that are counterproductive to getting me where I want to go?

How do I respond to problems? Am I only being reactive and looking for the quick fix? Or am I being proactive and looking for the underlying causes to find long-term solutions?

Have I ever felt like an impostor? Knowing what I know now, how would I feel and what would I do differently?

What is the one question I'm afraid to ask myself?

THREE

Who Are You and What Do You Want?

A ship in the harbor is safe, but that's not what ships are built for.

—William Shedd

Dissecting almost anything creates clarity but also poses a danger. Maybe you remember ninth-grade science class, when you were given the assignment of dissecting a frog. The purpose in school was to isolate and study the parts of the frog—muscles, bones, and organs—to learn how they worked together. When you touched a probe to a particular area, an eye would blink or a leg would move. It was an enlightening experience and resulted in a deeper understanding of a frog's anatomy. As you answer the questions using the prompts and guidelines in the next four chapters, you will see how each one is integrated with and complements the other three. The results, unlike the dissected frog, will create a living, breathing picture of knowing who you are and having what you want.

Defining Who You Are

Rachel Schreiber, a 26-year-old teacher in northern Virginia, is one person who had few doubts about who she was and what she wanted.

Although she had to cope with a learning disability, ADD, from the time she was a little girl, she dreamed about being a teacher.

"I always loved being at school—I liked the whole day itself and never wanted to leave. When I came home I'd teach my little sister, who was three years younger. I even made her do homework. I lined my stuffed animals up in my room as if they were students.

"Certain learning skills, such as reading, were tough for me. I would read a few pages, and then I'd have to go back to read them again because my mind would wander. In high school my science teacher told my mom that I was a very smart girl but was not doing as well as he knew I could. After looking at many options, we found that I was one of the fortunate students who benefited from medication for my condition, and immediately my grades went from Cs and Ds on tests to As and Bs."

Rachel, who now teaches in a public elementary school that has more than a thousand children, says that every day she has a story that reaffirms her choice to teach: "In such a large student population there are many children with learning disabilities. Take Danny, for example, who was eventually diagnosed with autism. Danny had been homeschooled until the first grade, and his parents said he had never really been around kids. Danny's first day of school also happened to be mine, so this became a real learning experience for us both. I had to figure out how to handle him, and he had to figure out how to handle himself. I had to take everything I learned in school and college and readjust my teaching to accommodate his needs. I came home every day very tired, and some days I just cried. But I knew this was what I wanted to do.

"It would have been so easy for me to walk into my principal's office and confess that I just didn't understand how to teach this little boy—and all these other children with other disabilities. But I knew I had to stay with it and help each and every one of them.

I did a lot of research on my own—and eventually wrote a book about working with the children at my school.

"But the real reward came on the last day of class that year, when Danny gave me a high five as we passed each other in the hall—and then I knew that I had finally gotten through. It brought tears to my eyes. I was proud to feel like I made a difference in his life."

As a child you, too, probably had lots of ideas about what you wanted to do when you grew up. Children's imaginations aren't restricted by the boundaries of age, inexperience, education, and parental control—they just imagine any future they want. But now that you are faced with the realities of adulthood, are you letting these restrictions stand in the way of doing what you want? Do you even share your goals with your spouse, boss, or friends? Or do you keep them to yourself because you fear what others' reactions may be? Worse still, do you let self-imposed boundaries—your lack of education, experience, or present circumstances—stop you from moving ahead?

The first step on this journey is to understand that these things do not define you or determine your future. You may have been asked the questions "Who are you?" and "What do you want?" in many ways and many times, but now is the time to tackle these questions seriously and to answer them in the way that will make sense to you.

What's Really Important?

Our society exerts constant pressure to be successful, which is why defining what success means to you is vital to your future. If you don't define success in your life, others will define it for you. You may find yourself climbing some ladder, only to discover that once you get to the top, it's leaning against the wrong wall.

Patrick Lencioni, the founder and president of the Table Group and author of bestsellers *The Five Temptations of a CEO* and *The Five Dysfunctions of a Team*, applies his core values in his own business when making decisions that have long-term impact on his organization—and on himself. "When demand for our consulting services went way up, we had a decision to make. People were encouraging us to grow, saying, 'You should be hiring more consultants!' 'You should be taking on more work!' 'You should be taking equity in your clients to share in their wealth because you don't know how long this is going to last!'

If you don't define success in your life, others will define it for you.

"I remember asking, 'What am I here for? What is the purpose of this company?' My family and my faith have to be more important than some pursuit of financial- or recognition-related goals. So my truth is that I should pursue those things—faith, family, and impact on people—and make a decision to forgo the lie, which is that money and fame and fortune and recognition will make me happy."

Aim for the Sweet Spot

In the life-planning workshops and retreats we lead, we help people prepare to answer "Who are you and what do you want?" with an exercise that will help them discover what we call their *sweet spot*. Try this: On a blank sheet of paper, draw three intersecting circles that overlap in the middle (see the following illustration). Label the first circle Strengths and in it write words that describe your talents, gifts, and abilities. Even include those that you may not be using now. In the second circle, labeled Passions, write the things that you highly value and are passionate about—the things that motivate you. Label the third circle Obligations and write in it the things that you are obligated to do to meet your needs and commitments. They may be fun or they may be hard, but you are doing them. With some reflection and analysis you may discover that some of these obligations are more necessary than others, and some may not be necessary at all. (You can figure out how to rid yourself of these unjustified obligations later on. For now, write everything down so you have a complete picture.)

The place where these three circles overlap is the sweet spot. When you are engaged in an activity or a job that uses your talents, ignites your passions, and fulfills your obligations, you're living in your sweet spot. The more these three circles overlap, the larger your sweet spot grows.

Are you using your strengths—your unique gifts and talents—to their fullest potential? Are you actively pursuing your passions or suppressing them? Do you feel content? Your passions and strengths are

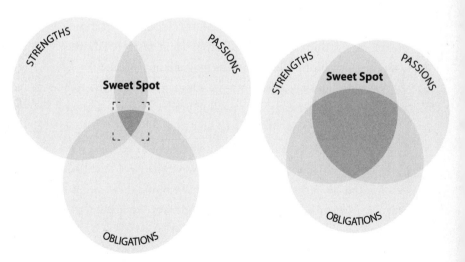

the clues to your personal destiny. The things to which you direct your attention grow stronger in your life—it's the simple law of attraction.

You can't control your strengths and passions; you can only develop them. That takes insight, intention, and discipline. Your obligations, however, are more flexible and can be altered more immediately. It is important that you take control of your obligations when you have the opportunity—or someone else will. If you don't decide how and where you will spend your time, talent, and energy, someone else will. Obligations are an important key to aligning your talents and passions and growing your sweet spot.

Playing to Your Strengths

In the 1940s George Reavis, a former assistant superintendent of the Cincinnati Public Schools, wrote a fable that illustrates the importance of playing to your strengths.[1] A précis of that story follows:

> Once upon a time the animals decided they must do something heroic to meet the problems of "a new world." So they organized a school.
>
> They adopted an activity curriculum consisting of running, climbing, swimming, and flying. To make it easier to administer the curriculum, all the animals took all the subjects.
>
> The duck was excellent in swimming, in fact better than his instructor, but he made only passing grades in flying and was very poor in running. Because he was slow in running, he had to stay after school and also drop swimming in order to practice running. This was kept up until his webbed feet were badly worn and he became only average in swimming. But because average was acceptable in school, nobody worried about that—except the duck.
>
> The rabbit started at the top of the class in running but had

a nervous breakdown because of so much makeup work in swimming.

The squirrel was excellent in climbing until he developed frustration in the flying class, where his teacher made him start from the ground up instead of from the treetop down. He also developed a charley horse from overexertion and then got a C in climbing and a D in running.

The eagle was a problem child and was disciplined severely. In the climbing class he beat all the others to the top of the tree but insisted on using his own way to get there. He was eventually expelled for being a troublemaker.

It's easy to be seduced by the promises of "You can have it all! You can do it all!" However, it's healthier to keep a realistic perspective. As that great philosopher Clint Eastwood said in the film *Dirty Harry*, "A man's got to know his limitations." You are more effective when you focus on and pursue the things you're skilled at—it's how your brain is wired. You can waste time, money, and energy pursuing unrealistic goals. As a woodworker might say, it's much easier to work with the grain than against it.

Our advice: don't abandon your dreams, but make sure your dreams are ultimately attainable with the talents and potential you already have.

Knowing Your Passions

Strengths don't always match up with our passions. But when you align your talents and enthusiasms, they support—even amplify— one another. You are more effective when they complement one another.

Dale Carlsen's passion drove him to open the first Sleep Train store in Sacramento, California. His company became one of the top three retailers in the United States and the recipient of countless honors and accolades from industry and government agencies not only for its business practices but for its contributions to social and community causes.

"Who would think anyone would be passionate about beds?" asked Carlsen. "I said it early on and repeated it often—my passion isn't mattresses, it's about people. Initially I wanted to help people get a better night's sleep for the best deal. I wanted to give them the answers to questions they haven't even thought about when they buy a mattress. I provide buyers with the kind of customer service that didn't exist when I got into the business. We needed to tell the customer why there were hundreds of dollars of difference between different beds. I am passionate about giving people information that can really have a positive impact on their mental and physical health."

Carlsen also says that one of his favorite parts of owning his company is helping his 1,400 employees find their passions too. "What is it that drives them? What excites them? You've got to really believe in what you are doing and believe in what you are trying to accomplish. What drives me now isn't to make more money or to open more stores. My passion is to watch my employees develop and become leaders."

Schedule Your Values

Although your talents and passions are there to be discovered and developed, you can control one area of your life starting this very moment. You can choose what you do with your time.

If you don't schedule your time, others will do so for you.

A professional office and home organizer we know often jokes, "Life is 90 percent maintenance and 10 percent fun." Although there is a lot to that statement, our intent is to help you balance those percentages. There are things that you can't avoid because they are part of the daily routine: buying groceries and preparing meals, keeping the household accounts, cleaning and laundry, mowing the lawn, getting the car serviced . . . the list is almost endless. Then you attend to your personal needs: exercising, journaling, talking on the phone, meditating, watching TV—which all take time and varying amounts of energy. All of these are tasks that you either do yourself or hire, train, and delegate others to do. Regardless, they all take big chunks out of your day.

The reality is that you can't do it all. You have to figure out your priorities, what you personally have to do, what you can get others to do for you, and what can go on your to-don't list!

One of the major course corrections you must learn is to determine the value of your time. This is key to aligning your obligations with your strengths and passions, thus enlarging your sweet spot. Like so many things in your life, if you don't schedule your time, others will do so for you. To have what you truly want, it is important to develop the habit of scheduling according to your values— do what is really vital to you first. Make sure your priorities are on your schedule before others fill it up with things that are not nearly as important to you. Don't fill your calendar with appointments and tasks. Schedule 20 minutes to do nothing in the afternoon; this will recharge your energy like nothing else.

Take a step back and look at this as an exercise in scheduling your values by answering these questions:

What do I want to be?

What do I want to do?

What do I want to learn?

With whom do I want to spend time?

Vicki Halsey is vice president of Applied Learning at the Ken Blanchard Companies. She is a presenter, keynote speaker, consultant, and coach for companies such as Nike, Toyota, Gap Inc., Merrill Lynch, and Wells Fargo. She is also coauthor of *The Hamster Revolution: How to Manage Your Email Before It Manages You*. Before Vicki joined the Ken Blanchard Companies, she worked in the education system.

"I was assistant school principal, serving on all kinds of committees and running administrative groups. All of a sudden I realized that I was killing myself. At the time I thought I needed to be defined by what I did. I was doing, doing, doing, and then I realized that's not what I wanted. I needed to be defined by who I am. I needed to be doing what I love—being with the kids. So I sat down and made a list of 16 things I was now doing that were not my core job. And within a 24-hour period, I resigned from 12 of those things.

"I didn't just abandon ship," she explains. "I reached out to people to fill those jobs. I found someone else for whom being able to teach a class at the California School Leadership Academy was the greatest gift of her life. Another person was so excited to take on the presidency of the school district's administrative group. Now I can do what actually strengthens me, and I feel like I'm doing what may be my greatest work."

The Clutter Factor

It's tough to have clarity with clutter in our lives. Clutter is like an overgrown garden. Only when you take time to pull the weeds will fresh ideas have a better chance of growing. Clutter is distracting and obscures the truth. Clutter accumulates gradually and is much worse than a single crisis that gets your attention immediately. Clutter overwhelms you slowly and lulls you into inertia. One year flows into two and then ten. Ask the employee who suffers from clutter, "How long have you been a manager?" He may say "Oh, ten years . . ." In reality he's been a manager one year, repeated ten times by filling his time with "clutter" but having no growth, learning, or progress. Distracted from using his strengths and engaging his passions, he has lost sight of the truth of who he is and what he values.

Make Your To-Don't List

Almost everyone has a to-do list. And it seems that we just keep adding and adding to our schedules. The trouble is that we don't subtract as fast as we add, and that kind of math doesn't work for human beings with finite capacities. Ron Heifetz, director of the Center for Public Leadership at Harvard University, says, "When you are engaging in any kind of strategy, you are really asking yourself to sift through what you are *not* going to do." Vicki Halsey made her "to-don't" list and you can, too. Give yourself permission not to do the items on your list. Focus happens only when you are not spread thin by overobligating yourself. The things that don't fit must be eliminated. *The secret of concentration is elimination.* People who achieve the most are determined *and* selective. Successful people declutter their lives. They get rid of the weeds that choke out their strengths and passions.

20 Will Get You 80

More than a hundred years ago, the Italian economist Vilfredo Pareto brought to light a principle that helps everyone achieve more with less effort. It's been referred to variously as Pareto's Law, the Law of Substitution, the Law of the Vital Few, the Principle of Least

Effort, and what is perhaps its best-known name, the 80/20 Principle. It simply states that 80 percent of your productivity is brought about by 20 percent of your effort. The percentages may change depending on what you're doing, but the formula shows the imbalance between what you do and what you get out of it. Well-placed effort can result in the best results and most of the rewards you want. If you look at it another way, most of your efforts in achieving what you want are irrelevant to what you truly want or value. Those fruitless efforts are only weeds in your garden.

What are the very few things that if done well can make the biggest difference in your life?

The goal is not merely to achieve what you finally want, but also to enjoy every step of the way getting there. It's not about enjoying only the result; it's about enjoying the process and the changes you discover in yourself as you move on. It's not a matter of putting up with drudgery until you eventually grab some gold ring at the end of the ride. As Warren Buffett says, "That would be like saving up sex for old age!" This is the essence of the 80/20 Principle, and only you can determine what the very few things are that if done well can make the difference in your life.

Balance Alone Is Not a Satisfying Goal

Balance started as a good concept, but it has become little more than a buzzword today. As an end in itself, it has no real advantage. Some use the term *balance* as an anesthetic to dull the pain of an empty life. It's possible to live a balanced life with all the parts in place and functioning and yet not have a clue who you really are or what you really want. Until you know what is valuable to you, what does having a balanced life really mean?

For Reflection

Assess your strengths, passions, and obligations in depth using the following exercises. Your answers are for you alone. There's no need to be self-conscious. Self-consciousness is what happens when you are too concerned about what other people think about you. Self-awareness, on the other hand, is to know yourself at the deepest level. And knowing yourself allows you to be in control of your life.

Look over all of the questions before you begin. Write your answers in your notebook or on your computer and date them. Review your answers a month from today.

My Strengths Assessment

When people are asked if they know their strengths, most respond immediately that they do. Yet when pressed, they are often at a loss to articulate them. The following questions will help you describe and understand your true strengths.

What have I done in the past that gave me a sense of satisfaction?

What are three things I do well?

What are my strengths? How do I use them?

What do others say are my strengths?

My Passions Assessment

A wise person once said, "While you're thinking, think big! You can always act small later." Even though the assessments of your strengths may reveal certain limitations, the real danger is putting limitations on your thinking. Be realistic but also recognize that in an attempt to be practical, you may often end up playing it too safe and developing imagination gridlock.

> What are the things I would like to do well?
>
> What are the experiences I would like to have?
>
> What do I want to start doing right now?
>
> What are five nonnegotiable values in my life?
>
> What things, events, or activities make me feel fully alive?
>
> What have I let slide? Why? What can I do now to reverse that?
>
> What would be my "perfect day" at work? At home?
>
> What would I do if I were guaranteed success in each of the various areas of life?
>
> Write a paragraph describing your life if you were using all your talents and abilities.

My Obligations Assessment

Most people use their schedules to let other people set their agendas. They are adapting their schedules to meet other people's expectations. Reflect on and answer the questions that follow. Your most powerful insights will be generated through reflection without any need for additional information. Your brain already has more information than you can imagine, and reflecting will bring your best ideas to the surface.

What is on my schedule that doesn't need to be there? What things can be abandoned or at least cut back? What obligations am I creating for six months from now that I will regret then?

Are any of the experiences that I would like to have that I listed in my Passions Assessment reflected on my schedule? Weekly? Monthly? Yearly?

What am I doing that I don't enjoy doing? What am I doing that I love to do?

What are the things other people want me to do? What are the things that I want to do?

What are some things I would like to do that fall under the category of "now or never"?

What is the 20 percent of my effort that produces 80 percent of the results I want to accomplish?

FOUR

Where Are You and Why Are You There?

We can easily forgive a child who is afraid of the dark; the real tragedy of life is when adults are afraid of the light.

—Plato

You're at a shopping mall to meet a friend for lunch at a place you've never been. You make your way through the labyrinth parking area and realize it's not going to be easy to locate the restaurant. The mall has hundreds of stores and a dozen corridors that all look alike. You find a directory and eventually spot the name. You realize you're still directionally challenged until you see that familiar dot that reads, *You Are Here.* You are relieved because now you know it'll be a lot easier to get to where you want with the perspective of where you are. Now plotting your course to the restaurant seems easy.

Where You Are and Why It Matters

Knowing your current location is essential to reaching your desired destination. If you try to download driving directions for a trip, the map service can't respond until you enter a starting point. It's easier to make decisions about your future once you know how your past and present connect to it. Like when you're looking at the directory map at the mall, you need some context. You need a larger picture so you can see where you are in relation to where you want to go. Context provides perspective. It helps show you the direction and how far you have to go. It is an indispensable part of the Four Questions because it leads to the next important part of your journey: choices and decisions.

Throughout your life you have made choices and decisions every day, which have put you where you are right now. You make your choices and decisions, and they make you. In assessing where you are and why you are there, you become aware of decisions you regret and wish you could do over and the ones that gave you great results that bear repeating. Some have been productive and others not so much. But before you can move forward, you have to first assess where you are and then examine the decision process that brought you there. Making a poor choice or decision is not the problem as much as not recognizing the connection between your current state and the choices and decisions that led you to where you are.

Interrogate Reality

For many individuals, decisions and choices tend to be unconscious. They feel that life happens to them. They don't see themselves as the architects of their own lives. Such a lifestyle can drain anyone of a sense of personal power, control, or confidence. They become stuck. As we said in the introduction, this leads to a regression of the imagination and the belief that things will always remain the same as they now are. Eventually it will affect their emotional and physical well-being.

Conversely, those who take the time to stop and reflect find it easier to direct their choices and decisions toward the life they want. They ask themselves questions—hard questions. And they give themselves honest answers. They interrogate reality.

> ## "You don't drown by falling in the water; you drown by staying there."
> ## —Edwin Louis Cole

The Reflection in the Mirror

One major reason why so many don't interrogate their reality is because they've never learned how to stop and reflect. Some fear reflection because this process can call up deep emotions that are connected with the past, wiping out a sense of control. And for some, believing that they are in complete control of their lives is paramount. Confident people, however, take the time to reflect. There is no real learning process, sense of discovery, or insight without reflection.

The word *reflect* in Latin means "to refold." When you look in the mirror the image goes in, refolds, and reflects. Personal growth comes when you use your mind's mirror. Taking the time to reflect on any circumstance or event in your life will bring you exciting new insights.

Reflection Is Not Simply Navel-Gazing

Reflection is different from introspection. Introspection is simply looking in. Stopping there limits your perspective or even diffuses it. It can lead some people to pessimism and even depression.

Reflection is looking in so you can look out with a broader, bigger, and more accurate perspective. Without reflection your life becomes subject to happenstance; you run through your days without gaining real insights. Day-to-day activities do not automatically become experiences. Asking "Where am I and why am I here?" initiates a reflective process. It shows you the red *You Are Here* dot on the map. Self-help is initiated in self-reflection, which leads you from where you are to where you want to go.

Closing the Integrity Gap

Often there's a gap between what people profess to believe and how they behave—it's called the integrity gap. Like all the areas of your life, integrity involves growth. The integrity gap narrows as you become more in sync with what you say you believe and how you behave. Your relationships, emotional well-being, and health are all affected by your integrity or lack thereof. Research shows that one's level of integrity actually strengthens or weakens the immune system. The more dissonance there is between your values and behavior, the more stress you experience, which weakens your immune system. The more alignment, the less stress and the healthier your system. Knowing where you are and why you are there helps close the gap.

Growing in integrity means becoming an authentic person. When you become the author of your life, you are authentic. You are not merely the shadow of what you could be. The shadow self is not what you were meant to be.

In business the term *organizational alignment* describes when employee actions match the values of the organization. But there's also personal alignment: making sure that your life actions are aligned with your values. There is a direct connection between who you say you are inside and what you're actually doing on the outside. To achieve alignment you're going to need a clear vision for your own life.

Jane Roeder, managing director of the Ukleja Center for Ethical Leadership at California State University, Long Beach, says that she was taught that thinking of herself was selfish, and she learned to put others ahead of herself. As a result it was hard for her to know who she was because she was defining herself in relation to what she did for others. This is an issue that she believes she shares with many women in particular.

"I started to have little churning feelings in my gut telling me there were things I couldn't ignore," she says. "My son Sean was in his first year of high school, where he was failing four subjects. Meanwhile I was working around the clock and was never at home. I looked at what I professed to be my priorities, my values in terms of family and being true to who I am. I thought, 'I'm out of integrity. I say that my family is first, but I'm putting my job first.' I wasn't living my values.

"I gave myself the gift of four months on personal sabbatical where I really focused and reflected on my purpose, my vision, my values, and my gifts. I asked myself, 'What do I want to do next?' I knew that to do a job search, I'd have to have some key words to define who I was. I did some personal assessment because I knew those words were going to be critical. After my personal retreat, the four words that I came up with were *leadership*, *education*, *nonprofit*, and *spirituality*. Now I have all four of those things at my new job at the Center for Ethical Leadership, located four minutes from my house, and now I can be home if Sean needs me."

Reflections from the Carnival

As children we loved going to the carnival. The fun house was particularly exciting. We would run through the maze of mirrors, not knowing which way to turn. We would leave with little knots on our heads and bruises on our knees from running down what we thought was a hallway only to run into an immovable glass wall. On the way out, the walls of the tiny lobby were lined with wildly curved mirrors with distorted images of the real us. The mirrors made us look tall and skinny or short and fat. Our faces looked warped: big ears, bulging eyes, large nose, and fat cheeks. We laughed and laughed because we knew what we saw was distorted— we knew it was not the real us, not the authentic us.

You have an internal mirror that reflects how you see yourself. What you see determines your behavior—often subconsciously. And when that image is distorted, it's not funny. Who you really are and what you really want can become minimized or exaggerated by what you believe about yourself. Without some honest self-reflection, you expend a lot of energy trying to find the right image to project to others. It's not about being perfect. It's about being honest. And when you find and hold an accurate image of yourself, that's when you'll experience a sense of well-being and authenticity. This is why knowing where you are and why you are there is so important in getting a more accurate picture of yourself.

It's not about being perfect. It's about being honest.

Jonathan W., who is now a successful executive search consultant, shared the story about his path to acknowledging and accepting himself for who he is—without distortion—and what he did with that knowledge.

"I hit the wall on February 29. When a good friend suggested

I look at an inpatient alcohol treatment facility, I was more than ready to try it. But wanted to do it now—before I changed my mind. Within three hours I was in a 12-step inpatient treatment facility, where I stayed for 28 days.

"Fundamentally what I learned was that alcohol was not the problem; I'm the problem. The alcohol was a means to numb the pain, which came as a result of my inability to know how to deal with life in any aspect: business, personal, or family. I was an emotional 14-year-old in a 31-year-old body. I had a lot of maturing to do. Only after I stopped the pain, learned to live in my own skin, and recovered physically and emotionally was I able to think about life's big essay question: 'What do I want?'

"When we were kids taking tests in school, everybody wanted the true/false, multiple-choice tests because they were easier. With an essay question we had to actually think. I had never really been forced to answer the essay question 'What do I really want to do?' I'd never been pushed to ask myself that. I was unprepared to answer it."

It took hitting the wall for Jonathan to face some things about himself that he needed to address, such as his problem with alcohol and what he wanted to do with his life. Once he did, however, he was able to take the next steps toward improving himself and living the life he really wanted.

What You See from Where You Are

There are four lenses through which you can gain perspective:

1. How others view you. The opinions of others tend to affect your behavior.

2. How you attempt to make others see you in a certain way—your image management to control first impressions.

3. The way you actually see yourself. You easily see your flaws and the things you'd like to change and are rarely satisfied with what you see.

4. Authentic self: made up of your loves, strengths, gifts, talents, abilities, passions, fears, hopes, and character. Any of these may be buried far below the surface of your consciousness.

The key to living a life of integrity is to bring these four lenses into alignment. And the key to that alignment is in discovering your authentic self. Being authentic means that you have a true picture of yourself and then express yourself congruently and consistently to yourself and to others. We use the word *congruent*, meaning that you are the same person no matter where you are. You are, as they say, "comfortable in your own skin."

Embrace Your Past

Knowing where you are and why you are there involves embracing the past. Accepting the things that happen *to* you is often much easier than embracing the things that happen *because of* you. Reflecting on the things that happen because of you can often lead to guilt, and as Erma Bombeck loved to say, "Guilt is the gift that keeps on giving." Guilt can lead to self-sabotaging behavior. "So what should I do with the failures in my life?" you may ask. Embrace them.

What successful person hasn't had a share of fumbles, trauma, disappointments, strategic upheavals, and failures?

The key player in counterproductive behavior is denial. The failures of your past should be acknowledged gently and lovingly—whether they were self-imposed or other-imposed. When the Center for Creative Leadership asked participants in their workshops to identify the things that contributed most to their development, the four most common factors were the following:[1]

Personal hardships	34%
Challenging assignments	27%
Mentoring relationships	22%
Structured training and assignments	17%

If success can be achieved in spite of—or perhaps because of—hardships and challenges—then why do organizations and people not learn from mistakes and failures? In a word: denial. People who are growing are not immune from problems; winning streaks are not trouble-free periods.

Understand Your Failures

Biosphere 2, built in the late 1980s in the foothills of Arizona, was designed to be an airtight replica of Earth's environment. The glass-and-frame structure seals in 7,200,000 cubic feet. It contains five different biomes, including a 900,000-gallon ocean, a rain forest, a desert, and agricultural areas, along with a human habitat. On September 26, 1991, a colony of eight people—four men and four women—entered Biosphere 2 with a mandate to live inside the dome for two years with no contact or support from outside. Several months into the first mission, the oxygen level began to fall at a steady rate, forcing the "bionauts" to have oxygen pumped in from the outside. The crew remained inside for two years, but the project lost credibility. The experience was not without valuable lessons, however. One interesting observation concerned wind and trees. There was no wind inside Biosphere 2, so the assumption was that the trees would grow quickly—and they did. But they kept falling over before their reproductive age. It appeared that wind was necessary for creating hardy and strong trees. After observation and experimentation, researchers determined that the lack of wind caused the wood to grow softer than trees of the same species growing in the wild. Although this appeared to be an advantage at first, in the long run the lack of pressure and conflict actually weakened them.

When you reflect on your life, you find that your personal hardships and business failures become key learning experiences. They can build your character and that of any organization. When you deny or ignore them, your authentic self doesn't have a chance to grow stronger and your future is sabotaged.

People are reluctant to make changes in their lives, as we discussed in Chapter 1. It feels safer than facing the fear of losing something they perceive as necessary in their lives. Woody Allen made the point in *Annie Hall*, quoting an old joke. A man enters a psychiatrist's office and says to the doctor, "Doc, my brother's crazy. He thinks he's a chicken." The psychiatrist replies, "Why don't you just have him committed?" The man replies, "I can't! I need the eggs!"

For Reflection

Take a look at the difference between what you say and what you do. Think back on your choices and decisions—the thoughts, behaviors, and actions that influenced you and got you where you are today.

Where do I feel stuck?

What truth about my life do I avoid exploring? Why?

What decisions and choices brought me to where I am today? Do I see a repeated pattern or theme? Would I repeat that today?

Who can give me feedback as I explore these questions?

FIVE

What Will You Do and How Will You Do It?

We are what we repeatedly do. Excellence then is not an act, but a habit.

—Aristotle

Planning.

Be honest with yourself. How did you react to that word?

Unfortunately many people seem allergic to the planning process and avoid it whenever possible. Why? Some believe that planning requires too much effort and that it takes too much time out of their already busy schedules. Others consider plans to be too inflexible and quickly irrelevant in a fast-changing world. Still others are afraid to enter into a planning process simply because they don't understand how to do it correctly. Whether or not you actually take the time to do it, planning the path to the rest of your life—the best of your life—is essential if you hope to have a chance of achieving what you want.

Mastering life requires understanding what is happening to you now, and then creating and using a plan for going from where you are today to where you want to be tomorrow. This is accomplished by asking the question, "What will I do and how will I do it?"

Problem or Predicament?

There is simply no avoiding it—storms in life will happen that will threaten to blow you far off course from your destination. But before you set about making your own course corrections, you have to understand that some of the things that you must address will be *problems*, and others will be *predicaments*. It is important that you know the difference between the two and how to deal with each, because each requires a different course of action.

A problem is a negative, unexpected event. It can happen through no fault of your own. For instance, a business competitor may introduce a new product or service that threatens your market share or your career. With clear thinking you will be able to see your way through most of these kinds of problems and learn from the experience. A problem can also be a mistake you make. You may have said something impulsively out of anger and frustration. Face the fact that you made a mistake; apologize as soon as possible, make amends, and be certain that you never repeat that mistake.

A predicament, on the other hand, is the result of a behavior pattern that keeps getting you into difficulty. For example, alcoholism, out-of-control spending, lying, cheating, procrastination, and other self-destructive behaviors and addictions can lead to predicaments such as the loss of your job, the disintegration of your marriage, bad credit, and poor health. Predicaments have symptoms that mask the core issue. Symptoms can appear as anxiousness, irritability, hostility, restlessness, sleeplessness, the inability to slow down, thoughtlessness, procrastination, inconsideration, depression, or debt. A predicament is the result of habitual behavior that

Mary Hunt is a good example of someone who turned a predicament into an asset. Her predicament started simply enough—getting one credit card, then more, and so on. Her out-of-control spending was literally mortgaging her family's future. The short version of her story is that once she realized that her self-worth is not dependent on her net worth—or what she could buy—she started the step-by-step 13-year process to pay off more than $100,000 in unsecured debt plus penalties and interest.

After attending one of Mick's leadership presentations, Mary felt encouraged enough to start the organization Debt-Proof Living, taking her well-earned credo public: "Bringing dignity to the art of living below your means." Her successful and beneficial organization is now reaching millions of people, helping them distinguish between their problems and their predicaments. Her honest message met with overwhelming success and has resulted in the release of her 14th book, *Live Your Life for Half the Price.* Today her website attracts more than 12 million hits a month and features Mary's constant themes of financial responsibility, empowerment, and hope.

has evolved into unconscious behavior. As time goes on, it becomes more difficult to recognize it for what it is.

Predicaments can be addressed and resolved, but not until the underlying cause is identified. A predicament becomes solvable by recognizing the issue for what it really is.

Answering the Question

Twenty years ago Trudy Atchison, a high school teacher who works with at-risk students, asked herself, "What will I do and how will

I do it?" She discovered that once she'd figured out who she was and what she wanted and where she was and how she got there, the answer to the third of the Four Questions that comprise the heart of this book was clear.

"My first attempt at a college education was in Philadelphia back in the late 1960s," she recollected. "The Vietnam War was going on, and it seemed war protests on campuses occupied the attention of most students. Everything, especially attending class, seemed so meaningless." Eventually Trudy dropped out of college and moved first to New York City, then to California.

"My first job in California was as a waitress at the original Brown Derby in Los Angeles," she recalled. "One day while working on the outside patio with another waitress who was at least 60 years old, I thought, 'Oh my, what if I'm still doing this when I'm 60?' At the time, I was enjoying the work, earning good money, and felt OK with my job. But it scared me to think of being a waitress all my life. Things were slow before the lunch crowd started to show up, so we began talking. I asked her, 'Did you always want to be a waitress?'

"She looked me in the eye and said, 'No. I didn't want to do this all my life, but this was the only job I could get. I don't have any education. What you need to do,' she said, '—and I give this advice to every young girl who works here—is think about what you really love to do, then do it. You'll always be doing something you really love, and it won't feel like work.'

"Several years later I was listening to a call-in radio show, and one of the callers said, 'I can't get a good job because I don't have an education.' The host said, 'You can go back to school; you can go to college. Even if it takes you 10 years, you can finish college if you go part-time at night. Many people have done it.' The caller said, 'Oh, I couldn't do that.' To which the host replied, 'What are you going to do in 10 years if you don't?'

"That really made me think that if I'm going to make the change, then I'm going to make it now. This is it. I was already in my forties.

"With the support of my family, I made immediate changes to cut down my expenses. I used my savings to pay off my credit card debt. I applied for every college grant and scholarship that was available. I took out student loans. I advertised for a roommate to use the spare bedroom. Eventually my daughter and I moved to a smaller place closer to my parents so my daughter would have supervision on the nights I attended classes.

"At one point I substituted in the juvenile court schools. I immediately realized that I had found an organization to which I wanted to devote my energies. I was impressed by the dedication and support that was given to students who were having difficulties, including teen pregnancy, gang involvement, anger management, drug and alcohol abuse, sexual abuse, abandonment, and homelessness. Working there was very rewarding, and eventually I was offered a contract. I was thrilled!

"When I look back I realize that all of my experiences, especially the jobs I'd had, helped me become a good teacher. I knew I'd be paying the loans off for quite awhile, but I believed it was a good investment. I was making an investment in me, not for something like a car that I would drive only for five or six years, but for me—permanently. I was investing in an opportunity to do what I loved.

"Everyone wakes up at a different time and in a different moment in their lives. Sometimes we have the fortune of getting advice from someone at just the right time—like the waitress at the Brown Derby who helped alter the direction of my life. I was ready to hear what she had to say, and now I have the best job in the world!"

Create a Plan for Life

In this chapter you'll learn how to create a plan for your life and how to deal with some of the obstacles you can expect to face. You'll know how to create your own agenda or road map for your life. And you'll be encouraged to write out that plan. (Studies show that putting plans into writing and reviewing them frequently increases the probability of achieving them by an average of 35 percent.) A written plan is not just something that's nice to do; it's an essential element in your success.

Planning is an essential tool that contributes to your long-term sense of well-being and fulfillment. Your ability to anticipate, take action, and capitalize on opportunities helps sharpen your skills and dramatically increases your probability of success—because you have a plan.

It is not surprising that we hear comments like the following from people who create and follow a plan for their lives:

"I'm glad I took the necessary time in the beginning because I saved many times over that in the end."

"I was surprised at how many problems I could handle along the way because I anticipated most of them ahead of time."

"It's amazing how many great new and unexpected opportunities came my way just because I had a well-thought-out plan and was able to articulate it."

Warning Signs That You're Not Planning

Maybe you think you're already doing a great job planning—and maybe you are. But are you really sure? Or is there room for improvement? You may have all the best intentions when it comes to planning, but if it's not happening, you're not growing. Here are several warning signs by which you can judge the effectiveness of your planning process:

When someone comes to you with an urgent problem, you often act before you have a chance to think.

You're bogged down in details with no time to look at the bigger picture.

There are too many options and you become confused about how to reach an outcome.

You're always busy putting out brush fires.

Others set your agenda and priorities for you.

The same issues and problems keep coming back, regardless of how many times you think you've solved them.

You're surprised when things don't go the way you expect.

When opportunities arise you're too busy to recognize or capitalize on them.

Why People Don't Plan

"I don't have time."

"By the time the plan's completed, it's already out-of-date."

"The process is too much work and it takes too long."

"I already have a plan—it's right here in my head."

Although people can come up with a whole host of reasons not to write out a plan for their future, two of the most common factors that get in the way of change are (1) fear (as we discussed in Chapter 1) and (2) the perception that there are no alternatives. We have observed over the years, perhaps surprisingly, that the perception of a lack of alternatives is by far the more debilitating. Fear can be overcome, but being unable to see alternatives causes people to become stuck and lose hope. When it comes to change, people need as much insight as possible. To help create alternatives for change, it is helpful when people understand the forces involved in change. Being able to identify these forces helps us overcome them. A great tool in understanding the forces involved in creating change personally or in groups is a system described as Force Field Analysis, developed by social psychologist Kurt Lewin.[1]

Real and lasting success doesn't happen merely by chance; it's the result of planned decisions and actions.

Any issue, be it a behavior, idea, or desired outcome, is held in balance—what Lewin calls *equilibrium*—by two opposing forces. The forces promoting change are held in equilibrium or balance by the forces maintaining the status quo. So your status quo behavior is not static; it is being held in place by opposite forces—the driving forces for change and the restraining forces against change. The forces are found in beliefs, cultural norms, values, expectations, behaviors, habits, moods, needs, anxieties, ideals, goals, and the like. They are pushing against each other to create your current state of being.

These forces are always at work in what Lewin referred to as *life space*—the place where people live their lives. These forces are a part

Typical Forces at Work

Driving Forces

- Felt need to change
- Negative consequences
- Personal crisis
- Advantages of change
- New opportunities
- Excitement
- Relational cohesion

Total

Restraining Forces

- Belief that things won't change
- Minimize consequences
- Overwhelming solution logistics
- Financial barriers
- Rigidity
- Apathy
- Conflicting needs of others

Total

THE CHANGE ISSUE

of all humans' lives, whether they recognize it or not. These forces never go away. Weakening or strengthening them is what shifts the equilibrium in one direction or another and produces change.

Force Field Analysis helps demystify change. It helps accurately describe the forces that are in effect when you attempt to make a personal change. With some thought, reflection, and a little analysis, you can begin to see clearly the forces, and once you identify them, controlling them is much easier.

In the model, if the restraining forces that push against change are equal to the driving forces that push for change, change will not occur. The forces for change must be stronger than the forces against change. The best way to create change is first to attempt to remove or weaken the restraining forces. If you weaken or remove the restraining forces, the result will be the desired change. When you are setting personal goals, the best way to create change is to first identify and then eliminate or weaken the restraining forces.

Putting It All to Work

To see how this works, following the model of Typical Forces at Work, take a sheet of paper and title it with a particular behavior you'd like to change. Then create two columns under the heading. In the left-hand column, list all the driving forces you can think of in favor of change. In the right-hand column, list the restraining forces, everything that prevents this change. See the following example that examines the all-too-common issue of trying to stop smoking.

As you fill in your own model, the following questions and statements will help you think through your desired change:

What do you want? What behavior do you want to change?

Where are you currently?

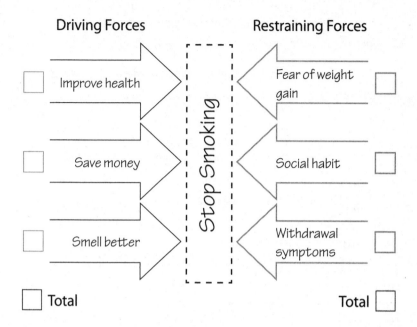

What will your life look like if you don't make the change?

What are the outcomes motivating you to change? List them in the left-hand column.

What are the factors making the change seem difficult? List them in the right-hand column.

Which driving forces are the most encouraging? Rate them on a scale of 1 to 5, with 1 being the weakest and 5 being the strongest, in the left-hand column.

Which restraining forces are the most difficult to overcome? Rate them on a scale of 1 to 5, with 1 being the weakest and 5 being the strongest, in the right-hand column.

How can you decrease or minimize the forces on the right and increase or maximize the forces on the left?

Which forces are real, and which ones are merely perceived to be real?

Now create your own chart. Write the issue that you want to change in the middle, between the arrows. List inside the arrows the forces for and the forces against change. Rate each on a scale of 1 to 5, with 1 being the weakest and 5 being the strongest. How can you weaken or even eliminate the restraining forces? How can you strengthen the forces for change?

Doing this exercise helps clarify how much the forces are at work in your environment and allows you more insight into how change can and will occur. You will find it more helpful when you can see the balance of power, the participants involved, your adversaries and allies, and your potential to influence all those forces.

This exercise will also help you identify the alternatives you have to bring about change in your life. It will also lessen your assumptions and your fear of change as you see more clearly all the issues involved. Because you now see the direction you need to go, it is easier to make a change that will take you where you want to be.

Turning Old Habits into New

One of the forces that may be working against you is old habits— things you do that hold you back. Although bad habits may be things that you fall into, good habits can be developed, and good habits beget positive attitudes, which beget new and satisfying life-styles. As you become more proficient with new behaviors, you'll find that they take less energy and effort. In the words of organizational visionary Max Depree, "We cannot become what we need to be, remaining what we are." Your new life plan demands new habits.

Catherine Kinney, former president of the New York Stock Exchange (NYSE), rose through the ranks at the NYSE holding management positions in several divisions, including technology planning, sales and marketing, operations, and regulation. During her career, her tremendous passion for the company has kept her going. "I have to pinch myself all the time because I am really surprised. I never would have expected to have had so long a tenure."

She knows that she got as far as she did because she made adjustments and improvements along the way. Those were part of her plan in achieving her goals. For example, several years ago during a performance review, she received some negative feedback. She could have become defensive or gone into denial, but she immediately accepted the information and created a plan to alter her behavior. Her challenge, interesting enough, was on the subject of change. We have rarely seen someone hit the mark so quickly and so surely. Here's her story:

"When we started doing 360-degree assessments I received feedback that I didn't manage change very well. That startled me because I always thought I contributed a lot to the change process and growth of NYSE, yet it was apparent that people saw me as part of the old school and a little resistant. It was just another reminder that you always have to be willing to be flexible.

"To make sense of this issue, I asked my supervisor to explain what was behind the scores. Then I went to two peers whom I really respect and asked them, 'What would you advise me to do?'

"I also approached two subordinates and said, 'Look, this can be challenging, so I don't want to put you on the spot. For the rest of this year, if you can point out to me moments when you think I am being inflexible, could you leave me a note? It doesn't have to be signed. It will be particularly helpful to me if you give me feedback that's in the moment and really concrete.' Instead of being resistant I try to work on being more flexible and to be seen as really trying to be part of a process of change."

Once Catherine had isolated the problem, she dealt with it by putting a system in place that could help train her to catch herself being less open to change. In the process she changed her behavior, positively influenced the opinion of others toward her, and no doubt was an inspiration to those around her.

Making New Behaviors Automatic

The more you rehearse your new behaviors by putting them into practice, the quicker and easier it will be to adopt them permanently. Ready to start?

1. Pick a specific new behavior that you want to turn into a habit. Express it in writing in the present tense, as if you are already doing it. Let's say, for example, that you want to spend more time with your family. A positive way to practice this new behavior would be to write, "I organize my work day well, and leave the office every day by 6:00 p.m."

2. Repeat your written goal and visualize yourself doing it. Be positive, be excited. You are programming your subconscious mind.

3. Commit yourself to your new behavior by doing it whenever appropriate.

4. Let others know that you are committed to a new behavior and encourage them to give you feedback.

5. Keep track of your progress on a daily basis. Celebrate and keep on doing what you're doing!

Why Set Goals?

A plan is simply a way to achieve specific goals you set for yourself. If you want to lose 5 or 50 pounds, you set that goal and then put the plan into motion by placing your new exercise and weight loss routine into your daily schedule. If your goal is to buy a new home, your plan begins by determining your sources of income for what it will cost and how to get the money you need.

You can choose to be casual and nonspecific about setting your goals, but the vaguer you are the less chance there is that your dreams will become a reality.

Goals are important stepping-stones in your journey to self-leadership because they:

- **Provide direction.** To get something done, have a clear vision of what your future looks like.

- **Tell you how far you have traveled.** Goals provide milestones along the road to accomplishing your vision.

- **Help make your vision attainable.** By breaking your plans down into smaller steps or tasks that—when accomplished individually—add up to big results, goals help make your overall vision attainable.

- **Give you something to strive for.** It's a fact: people are more motivated when challenged to attain a goal that is beyond their normal level of performance.

Step-by-Step Toward a Goal

Football placekicker Rolf Benirschke is one of the most beloved San Diego Chargers of all time. He played 10 seasons in the NFL before retiring at that time as the third-most-accurate kicker in NFL history. He is one of only 33 players to date to be elected to the Chargers Hall of Fame. For Rolf, however, the challenges of a life-threatening illness are almost as well chronicled as his exploits on the gridiron. Overcoming them took step-by-step determination to reach a goal.

"In my second season I was misdiagnosed with Crohn's disease," Rolf says. "Four surgeries and four years later it was determined my condition was colitis, not Crohn's disease. But during that time I got sicker and sicker, though I continued to play. I finally collapsed and had the emergency life-threatening surgery that turned me into a shell of my former self. I was convinced that my career, and more seriously my life, was over."

"I discovered who I was and what I wanted, at a deeper level than ever before." —Rolf Benirschke

----

"During one of my lowest points, one of my teammates, Louie Kelcher, went to coach Don Coryell and told him that they wanted to make me honorary captain for the day. That meant I'd have to walk out on the field for the coin toss. I wasn't sure I could. Louie said, 'If you can't walk we'll just have to carry you.' So we got to the sidelines, they called for the captains, and we started walking on the field. When my name was mentioned everyone in the stadium stood and cheered.

"It was overwhelming. By the time I got to midfield I was in tears. That is when I discovered who I really was and what I wanted, at a deeper level than ever before. In my mind I quit 100 times; my will kept going.

"Later on, the trainer coach for the team called and said, 'Let's get you back into shape.' And that was the beginning of my long journey back to the field.

"If I were to ask myself—and I did quietly—the rational question, 'Do you ever think you will play football again?' the answer would have been overwhelmingly 'There's no chance that I will ever play again with these bags on my side, with my cut-up stomach, weighing 123 pounds. It's over.' But I didn't accept that. I simply asked myself, 'How do I get through the day?' My mother used to say, 'Rolf, don't look at the top of the mountain; just understand it takes little steps to get there. Keep your head down.'"

Rolf played seven more years, and in a 1982 playoff game against the Miami Dolphins he kicked the winning field goal in one of the most exciting games in NFL history.

Promise Maker Versus Promise Keeper

When psychologists A. C. Ratzin and D. Payne did research on New Year's resolutions, they discovered that people make the same resolution over and over again.[2] On average, people resolve to stop a particular bad habit 10 times. But a promise maker does not a promise keeper make. After the first week, 25 percent of the research subjects gave up. After six months, 40 percent had broken their vows. The key to successful promise keeping is to set goals that can be broken down into doable steps.

"The secret to change is one step at a time."
—Mark Twain

What is it that you need to do this year—the thing that you have delayed and you're in danger of letting roll over into next year? What are you waiting for? Are you procrastinating? Maybe you need to go to somebody and ask for forgiveness. Maybe you need to go to somebody and offer forgiveness. Don't carry resentment, grudges, guilt, or bitterness to the next year. What are those key areas that will contribute to where you want to be?

SMART Goals Made Easy

The best way to setting goals is to do so in an organized, systematic way. In the bestselling book *Putting the One Minute Manager to Work*, Ken Blanchard and Bob Lorber describe the five most important characteristics of well-designed SMART goals:

Specific. Your goals must be clear and unambiguous.

Measurable. If you can't measure it, you can't manage it.

Attainable. Successful people set goals that stretch them.

Relevant. It's great to have goals, but only if they support your personal vision of the future.

Time-bound. Goals without deadlines are dreams, not reality.

Having too many goals can be overwhelming. You are far better off if you set a few significant goals and then concentrate your efforts on attaining them. When it comes to setting goals, less is more.

(For more about SMART goals, see Exercise 9 in the 48-Hour Personal Retreat at the end of this book.)

Creating a Learning Agenda

If there is a gap between what you know or the skills you have and the information or skills you need, create a learning agenda for yourself.

The following five steps can help you:

1. Determine your goals and ask yourself: Where do I want to be next year and in the years that follow? What do I need to do to accomplish those goals? Your answers instantly become your learning agenda.

2. Assess the skills or knowledge you'll need. Although some of your goals won't require new skills or knowledge, others will. What specific skills and knowledge do you need to have in order to achieve your goals? What main skill that you already possess would you like to improve by 25 percent within the next year?

3. Explore the best sources. That may mean going back to school for an advanced degree, enrolling in training offered by your employer, or developing relationships with mentors or coworkers who can teach you the ropes. There is an optimal source for every skill you decide you need to learn.

4. Create your learning agenda. Once you've gathered all your information, create your learning plan, one that lays out the skills and knowledge you need to acquire, along with where and when you'll go about it. Put your agenda in writing.

5. Execute. The fun begins—you get to put your learning agenda into action. The sooner you get going, the sooner you'll learn the skills and knowledge you'll need to enjoy and achieve your goals!

For Reflection

Writing down plans and setting goals are the most reliable way to move from your current reality to where you want to be. Your future is up to you. Begin your planning process by considering the following:

1. What would I like to do that I'm not doing now?

2. How might I proceed to change an old habit that does not serve me in a way that assures my success?

3. What are the restraining forces that hinder my progress?

4. What are the driving forces that will help me follow through on my goals?

5. What are three habits that will help me get where I want to be?

6. What skills would I like to improve during the next year? How can I do that?

7. Set three goals in your life: one each for your work life, your family life, and your personal life. Make sure they are Specific, Measurable, Attainable, Relevant, and Time-bound.

SIX

Who Are Your Allies and How Can They Help?

Two are better than one, because they have a good return for their work: if one falls down, his friend can help him up. But pity the man who falls and has no one to help him up!

—Solomon

Gentlemen, I don't want to hear what we can't do. I want you to tell me what we can do—and failure is not an option." Gene Kranz, flight director of NASA's Mission Control, spoke in a firm, measured voice to the room full of engineers after an explosion crippled the *Apollo 13* spacecraft. His sobering words galvanized four teams into action to save the lives of three astronauts hurtling through space two hundred thousand miles away.

It's hard to imagine a more complicated set of problems in a more critical situation. On board the *Apollo* craft, an electrical short had caused an explosion in the oxygen tanks. Jack Swigert, feeling the explosion and seeing a warning light blink on, delivered one of the most eloquent SOS calls of all time: "Houston, we've had a problem here." More warning lights turned on, signaling the loss of two of the three fuel cells as gas—oxygen—began escaping from the second and last tanks. The failures multiplied; the craft lost electricity, light, water, and power, and those were merely the most comprehendible of the myriad technical issues. Any prospect of a lunar landing was rendered impossible.

Back in Houston, Kranz's White Team at Mission Control was about to be relieved from monitoring the mission by the Black Team, directed by Glynn Lunney, when the "problem" occurred. Kranz, "boss of bosses," immediately reorganized the schedule so that Lunney's Black Team, Gerry Griffin's Gold Team, and Milt Windler's Maroon Team began to monitor the mission, while his White Team became the offline Tiger Team to focus, analyze, and offer solutions. Kranz then focused on keeping the exhausted, dehydrated crew awake as much as possible in the cold, darkened craft as he shifted the mission from a lunar landing to survival and return.

The four teams collected duplicates of every tool, material, and piece of equipment to be found on the capsule in a room, and, working with the astronauts, they came up with a plan that saved the lives of the *Apollo 13* astronauts: James Lovell, Jack Swigert, and Fred Haise. This incredible display of imagination could never have come from a single individual. It was the synergy among dozens on the ground and three astronauts in space, making the whole greater than the sum of its parts. Against all odds, *Apollo 13* returned and landed safely in the Pacific Ocean 88 hours later.

The following day President Richard Nixon awarded Kranz and the three other flight directors the Presidential Medal of Freedom. Two weeks later they followed the astronauts in a ticker-tape parade in Chicago.

Kranz's demands of his engineers, put into such powerful yet vulnerable language, rallied a diverse group of experts to strive in the face of the overwhelming odds. Commander Lovell later cred-ited Kranz's ability to surround himself with good people with the lifesaving success. "Kranz didn't have the answers. But he was able to leverage the strengths, insight, and wisdom of those around him to avert disaster."

Too often, instead of enlisting help, we are more concerned with how we believe others will perceive us if we ask for help. Does ask-ing for help indicate you're in trouble, that you're going under, or that you're weak and in a particularly vulnerable, dire state? Does it mean you can't take care of yourself or didn't prepare enough? If you were drowning in the ocean, would you call out to a lifeguard for help or berate yourself for all the swimming classes you didn't take? Or wonder what the lifeguard might think about the dire situation you're in? No question. You'd signal for help and not care one iota about much of anything else. When you're drowning in a problem, by all means ask for help! And as with the lifeguard, you trust others to use the skills they have honed to be useful and helpful.

When is the last time you heard anyone say that they learned and experienced all they could in order to hoard the information and keep it for themselves? Everyone loves being asked for advice because it's an honest compliment, a way of saying, "I trust you, I admire what you have accomplished, and you know more than I do!" Who wouldn't like to know that?

Success Isn't a Solo Act

Although your journey may appear on the surface to be a solitary one, this is not the case. Life is filled with *Apollo 13* "We've had a problem" scenarios, some major, some minor. It's up to us to be ready for everything and anything that comes our way.

Surrounding yourself with good people and mutual supporters

is a sign of strength. Achieving the life you want often requires the physical, emotional, psychological, and spiritual support of your family, friends, work associates, mentors, and everyday acquaintances. Mutual support allows you to achieve far more than you ever could on your own. The key to having the support you want is trust. And trust is a two-way street. In order to trust others, you must be trustworthy. When others trust you, they are usually willing to be there for you, too. Think of it this way:

Keep Simple Agreements + Do No Harm = Trust

The first part—keep simple agreements—means doing what you say you're going to do. If you make a promise to someone and honor that agreement, you strengthen the bond of trust with that person. Break or recklessly postpone a promise and you break a bond. Trust can build for years and evaporate in the blink of an eye. Trust is like a pure mountain stream with a fragile ecological balance.

The second part of the formula—do no harm—means that you won't take advantage of someone's vulnerability when that person places trust in you. It also means that when you trust someone else, you have no pretenses or false fronts. When you trust that someone will tell you the truth, and that this truth will not be used against you, both of you become better for the experience.

Plant Seeds of Trust

Behavior that promotes trust in relationships embodies five qualities: vulnerability, information sharing, empathy, celebration, and encouragement.

Vulnerability: People are drawn to your humility when you let them know you need them.

Information sharing: Whenever you share information about yourself with a trusted friend, you are creating an ally.

Empathy: The ability to listen, to understand, and to be sensitive to others' experiences and feelings is the mark of a mature person.

Celebration: In a trusting environment, friends celebrate each other's achievements as their own.

Encouragement: Long after you have forgotten your words or notes of encouragement, they are remembered by the recipient.

"I will never get from others what I myself am unwilling to give."
—Mike Scioscia

Mike Scioscia, manager of the Los Angeles Angels of Anaheim, knows this well. A major-league catcher for 15 years, he was twice a World Series champion with the Dodgers. He was selected as Manager of the Year in 2002 when he led the Angels to their first World Series championship. No one would have predicted this success from the way the team started its season. The Angels began the year by stumbling to a 6–14 start—not exactly a championship march.

"We all have blind spots," Scioscia says. "The successful person gathers all the information he can, even if it's uncomfortable, even if it's not what we want to hear."

Scioscia is an excellent communicator and doesn't consider vulnerability and transparency to be signs of weakness. For him they are a major source of strength and essential for his role as a leader.

As a result his team trusts him and his philosophy. "People have to feel your support and believe that they are something special, or they'll never reach their potential. That's what I want from those supporting me. I will never hope to get from others what I myself am unwilling to give."

It's a simple transaction—you know the formula now: keeping simple agreements plus doing no harm yields trust.

A Lesson from "The Fish"

Trust is the key to mutual support and allows you to achieve far more than you ever could on your own. Antwone Fisher had a difficult time trusting anyone. His mother gave birth to him while she was in prison. His father was shot and killed before Antwone was born. His foster parents mentally and physically abused him over a 14-year period. He eventually graduated from high school and joined the navy, where he received psychological counseling because of a deep-rooted anger-management issue. The very ideas of trust, mutual supporters, allies, or asking for help—let alone pursuing one's dream—were foreign to Antwone. It seemed that if he ever trusted anyone in his life, he was quickly punished for it.

While Antwone was in the navy, his psychologist noticed that he had a real talent for writing. He challenged him to develop those strengths and to get in touch with the passions deep within him. Antwone's counselor began to instill a sense of trust in him. It was a huge step for Antwone, but he began asking himself who his allies were and how they might help. Mutual supporters were beginning to emerge. Someone even paid his salary for nine months so he could write his autobiography, which became the bestselling book *Finding Fish: A Memoir* and the film that bears his name. Since then Antwone has become a successful author and screenwriter.

At a standing-room only lecture to 1,500 students at California

State University, Long Beach, Antwone emphasized the importance of having mutual supporters. "Look around," he said, "because you're here in part because of mutual supporters." He paused and continued, "Some of you were born on third base. Others on first base. It doesn't matter. You can't help where you start. The question is, what have you done with what you've been given?"

Sadly, studies show that most people focus on what they don't have rather than on what they do have. Accept where you are and build from there. Antwone wasn't on third base or first base. In fact he wasn't even in the ballpark. Yet he made it to home plate in part, by his own admission, "because of mutual supporters."

Winning with People

David Shakarian is a man many would consider to be a business legend. He is the founder of the General Nutrition Corporation (GNC). Today GNC has more than six thousand stores in the United States and 49 other countries. While Mick was in his mid-twenties, he had the privilege of observing David's business acumen and was enormously influenced by his perspective on relationships.

David told Mick, "Skills and habits are extremely important in building a successful life and sustaining a life mission, but in addition you must consider the people with whom you are surrounded." His success as a businessman was quite impressive. But it wasn't only his business savvy that continued to influence Mick's life. It was David's ability to focus on the key relationships that were needed to support his quest for who he was and what he wanted, both professionally and personally. His principle was simple: "The quality of your life will be in direct proportion to the types of relationships you choose to build." Relationships can help or hinder you. They will help you endure distractions on your journey, or they can be distractions.

One of the great slogans a few decades back was "You are what you eat!" which was also a favorite saying of David's. It's a physical truth; you can quantify it. But David took it one step further when he said, "You are who you eat with. Eating the right kinds of foods is important, but so is engaging the right kinds of friends. This must be intentional."

During our teenage years we spend one-third of our time with friends. As we grow to adulthood, work, family, and personal interests increase, and the average time we spend with our friends drops to less than 10 percent. If this is true for you, think about the friends with whom you want to spend that time. Are you seeing them? Pick your friends well and give them your prime times. How do your friends affect your personal and work life? How do they affect your other relationships? If you put all your friends in a room, would they all enjoy the time together? Why? Would you? Why? What do your friends provide you, and what do you offer them in return?

Have a Mentor, Be a Mentor

We all need a trusted counselor and guide, and at some point we all need to be one. We need mentors because of the perspective they provide. That perspective is evident in the roles that mentors play in our lives.[1]

Upward Mentors: These are the people to whom you look up. They have helped and are still helping you become who you are. They can be a parent, grandparent, coach, author, pastor, rabbi, or boss. They may be someone you haven't met.

Friendship Mentors: These are the people with whom you experience life. You have gone through various stages with them—college, career, or family and work life. They are your peers, and you've learned from them in a mutually giving way.

Sandpaper Mentors: You don't have to look for them; they always find you! These are people who rub you the wrong way. Don't reject all that they say simply because they are critical or cranky. In reality they can help you—if you are observant, open, and nondefensive.

Downward Mentors: These are the people in whom you are invested. They may be younger than you, but not necessarily. When you invest in others in a giving relationship, you actually learn a lot about yourself. You experience what's important to you and what should be emphasized and reinforced in your own professional and personal life.

Providing You with Instruction and Inspiration

Friends and mentors are the people who bring out the best in you. They are not afraid to tell you the truth. They keep you growing and on track. When you share your goals with them, they, too, are committed to those goals and become actively involved in your efforts. They act like a coach, giving you instruction to stick with your game plan, to perform at your peak. No matter what success you experience, your need for coaching will never diminish.

LeBron James is an extremely successful NBA basketball player. Does he have a coach? Perhaps several? Celine Dion, Barbra Streisand, and Beyoncé Knowles can sing circles around hundreds of other female singers. Yet each woman spends great time and effort to make sure she has the right voice coach. In fact, all professionals in all sorts of fields have coaches. That's why they're pros! Successful people at all levels make a habit of sharpening their skills

----

Successful people at all levels make a habit of sharpening their skills by surrounding themselves with those who can provide instruction and challenge their wits.

----

by surrounding themselves with those who can instruct and challenge them.

Benjamin Franklin produced his greatest inventions after he was 70 years old; he was still accomplishing much well into his eighties. He invented the iron furnace stove (called the Franklin stove), bifocal glasses, and swim fins; created the first library in the United States and a library system that is still in place today; and organized the first fire department, which had as its slogan "An ounce of prevention is worth a pound of cure." Franklin started a fire insurance system that protected businesses and homeowners and became world-famous for demonstrating the connection between electricity and lightning. He credited much of his productivity to the inspiration of the circle of people he called his "most ingenious friends group" who kept him growing and thinking.

Thomas Edison had his "mastermind alliance." It wasn't Edison who had the main idea behind the lightbulb. It was his alliance. They averaged one minor invention every six weeks and one major invention every six months. They came up with more than three hundred inventions in just six years. Friends inspire us. Ralph Waldo Emerson said, "A true friend is somebody who can make us do what we can." They bring out the best in us. They stretch us, press us, nudge us, and don't allow us to stagnate.

Major League Baseball's Pat Gillick, who is the general manager of the Philadelphia Phillies and former general manager of the Seattle Mariners, told us, "You can only accomplish so much. To go beyond your own limitations, you need help. You get that help from those surrounding you: your friends, associates, team, and significant others. So in a way they are as responsible for your success as you are."

The quality of your life will be in direct proportion to the types of relationships you choose to build.

One supporting friendship is worth a thousand acquaintances. The other side of the coin is also true. Nothing will sabotage your journey for the best of your life as quickly as the *wrong* friends. The quality of your life will be in direct proportion to the types of relationships you choose to build.

Dependence, Independence, and Interdependence

Many tests measure what is called synergistic decision making—the difference between individual and group decision making. In most cases, the ability to make good decisions—decisions that are based on accurate information and are also right for you—strengthens when you make them as a member of a group.

As human beings we were designed to be interdependent with those around us. At NASA, Gene Kranz's group of engineers wasn't *suddenly* interdependent when there was a potential disaster; he built a great team over time to be ready for anything. That's the way he functioned as launch director during the uneventful moments. In fact, if interdependence hadn't already become his normal mode of operation, it would never have worked in the crisis.

Think about the day you got your first driver's license. Getting that little laminated sandwich of paper and plastic was your first, official emphatic symbol of independence. But although you may have considered your driver's license a gateway to a new freedom from family and a way of staying out late with your friends, you actually entered into a thoroughly interdependent experience. You didn't just get in the car without someone first designing and making that car; another person sold it to you or your parents. Meanwhile, its fuel came from wells and refineries thousands of miles away. Your local utility company made sure stoplights in your neighborhood worked, and your town engineers (ideally) repaired the potholes. You were also dependent on all the other drivers on the road with you. If another driver ran a stoplight and crashed into your car or a pedestrian jaywalked in front of you, it quickly became apparent just how interdependent you were with the world around you.

Just as in driving, when we understand interdependence and embrace our supporters and mentors, we experience a more successful and enjoyable lifestyle.

The Final 10 Percent

People cannot grow without feedback. So why do so many avoid it? Simple—because feedback can be painful. Hearing the truth about ourselves is simultaneously difficult and rewarding. Most people will tell you 90 percent of what you need to know. That's the easy portion. It's that last 10 percent that makes the biggest difference. You don't necessarily want to hear the bad news, nor do others want to take on the burden of sharing that news. That's where the cultivation of trusted friends pays great dividends. They must be invited in by you. They won't volunteer for this hazardous duty without incentives from you. As King Solomon said, "The wounds of a friend are more faithful than the kisses of an enemy."

"Sometimes the very thing that seems to derail us is the catalyst that keeps us on track."
—Pat Gillick

Pat Gillick, vice president and general manager of the Philadelphia Phillies, says, "Baseball is very much a people business. To be effective, baseball players need to know where they stand in their organizations, and they have to be able to completely trust their managers and teammates. This means being as honest and as open as possible.

"About 40 years ago when I was playing in the minors I asked the general manager what my chances were of going into the big leagues. Even though it wasn't comfortable, he was pretty frank with me. 'I would say that you have a slight chance,' he said, 'but in reality not a very good chance of making it to the majors.'

"That stung. And even though it immobilized me for a time, I knew it was true! Looking back, denying the truth about myself would have handicapped my future success. At that point I made a decision to go to some other aspect of the game. After assessing my skill set along with my passion for baseball, I decided to get into the administrative side of the game. My manager's honest feedback and my willingness to listen eventually opened up a whole new direction for my life. Sometimes the very thing that seems to derail us is the catalyst that keeps us on track."

Knowing who you are and having what you want won't happen without understanding that help from your allies includes honest feedback.

"One of the keys to my success is to surround myself with people who can give me honest feedback," Pat says. "Detractors are not invited into that circle. I look for mutual supporters. I also look for those people I can learn from, who are in a position to mentor me."

People Don't Know What They Don't Know

If you are not honest with who and where you are, you will never arrive at where you want to go. Feedback about performance and potential is one of the most critical components of personal and professional growth. Nothing happens until growth-minded people gather direct, timely feedback on the things that really matter. But it's not enough to surround yourself with good people—you must be one yourself.

Discovering who you are in relation to others is a key step. One helpful tool for that purpose is the Johari Window, a graphic model of interpersonal awareness developed by psychologists Joseph Luft and Harry Ingham.[2] It is a model of interpersonal processes that illustrates relationships in terms of awareness and identifies four distinct areas based on oneself and others. The following chart, based on the Johari Window, describes these interpersonal relationships in similar fashion.

Open and Authentic: All people's lives have an open area. You may be completely comfortable with transparency in a certain area of your life, such as talking about your relationships, money, or

Open and Authentic What you see is what you get. I know myself and allow others to know me exactly as I am.	**Blind Spots** What others see in me but I don't or can't see about myself
The Secret Self What I know about myself and what others don't know about me	**Unknown Potential** What others don't see in me and I don't yet know about myself

your goals. (Most people have some aspect of themselves, however mundane, about which they'll be readily candid.)

Blind Spots: Blind spots are evident in behaviors that others see but of which you may be unaware. It's like having bad breath or spinach in your teeth: everybody knows it but you. For example, you may see yourself as being easygoing, but others may sense an intensity of which you are not aware.

The Secret Self: Your secret self involves what you avoid revealing to others—your little secrets or skeletons in your closet. It could be something serious that if known could get you fired, divorced, or bankrupt. Or it may be information about yourself that you are sensitive or embarrassed about.

Unknown Potential: This is also the area of potentially your greatest growth. This is where much of your untapped potential lies dormant. However, neither you nor others are aware of this.

Self-talk is the internal dialogue going on in every person's hidden area. Although other people's input is influential, the input you give yourself has even more impact. During stressful, anxious times the input can be negative or deceptive. Alternately, it is easy to engage in pipe dreams, rooting your internal dialogue in illusion. What we've found is that most people's internal dialogue does not reflect reality. Reality-based self-talk, however, deals honestly and objectively with what's going on.

Discovering the Whole Person

The key to understanding all of the parts of the Johari Window is the open area. As the open area expands, you have fewer blind spots, less hidden area, and less unknown area. There is more congruity and alignment in your life. That's when you become whole. That's when the idea of who you want to be more closely matches who you are.

You can't deal with the blind, hidden, or unknown areas without other people in your life. Dealing with those areas requires feedback that is both truthful and candid from mutual supporters. And those relationships are based on trust. Exposure is not easy; without trust, it won't happen. When you tell others your dreams, your true desires, your goals, and your vision for the future, invite feedback. And remember the 90/10 rule mentioned earlier in this chapter. That final 10 percent is crucial information—look for it and welcome it! It can be one of your greatest sources of personal growth, but hearing it takes trust, courage, and the smart person to encourage that information!

The only thing standing in the way of 100 percent disclosure is fear. Just as fear can be a roadblock to change, it can be both pervasive and poisonous and is antithetical to the best qualities of human nature. Candid and honest information you get from others can be painful because you often see yourself differently than others do. But after you get over the initial shock, you will have a much more realistic picture of yourself and understand how this information will be invaluable to getting to where you truly want to go.

Touched by an Angel

It's a Wonderful Life is a beautiful story about the priceless value of relationships. Jimmy Stewart's George Bailey is a man who has done so much for so many. He has invested in the lives of people— so much so that he sacrificed travel and adventure to do it. His father had died suddenly and he took on the responsibility of the family business. The town needed him as president of the savings and loan.

During the film we get to know George from his head to his heart. We see how he was shaped in his younger years from a boy through adolescence to become a husband, father, and business owner. His humanity and humanitarianism are magnetic. His interests always seem to take a backseat to the needs of others. But as his frustration mounts, you see it in his moods. His self-talk becomes more negative by the moment, yet he doesn't realize it. He feels stuck in his little town of Bedford Falls when he assumes the rest of the world has so much more to offer. His work hours are long and tedious; other people tug on his coattails, looking for him to solve their problems. And what does he get in return? His salary is modest, and he's living in a humble house in desperate need of repair.

When bankruptcy threatens the business, he comes to the brink of a nervous breakdown and he decides to throw himself off a bridge into the dark, cold waters below.

But Clarence, his guardian angel, embodied as a lovable, befuddled old man, jumps first, because he knows that George won't let him drown, and in the act of saving Clarence, he'll save himself. Clarence then gives George a glimpse into the past and future to see what the lives of others would be like without him. With that perspective, George comes to realize that his life is indeed worth living.

George arrives home only to discover that all those relational deposits he's made over the years have come back in an outpouring of generosity and support for him. His friends, neighbors, and business associates have taken up a collection that secures his business and saves his future. Then George discovers a note left behind by his guardian angel: "Remember, George: no man is a failure who has friends."

For Reflection

Surrounding yourself with good people, business colleagues, friends, and mentors takes a discerning eye, and it requires trust. To gain the trust of others, you must yourself be worthy of their trust. Build a strong group of mutual supporters by answering these questions:

Who are my allies? How can they help me accomplish my goals?

Who can help me see my unknown potential?

What is my system for exposing my blind spots that slow my progress?

What resources do I need to accomplish my goals?

What people are crucial to my success? Are they on my team?

SEVEN

Knowing Who You Are and Having What You Want

We don't see things as they are; we see them as we are.

—Anaïs Nin

Are you ready to begin your journey to the best of your life? It's easy to lose sight of your destination. There are countless options, distractions, turns, and unexpected detours that can take you toward or away from where you want to go. Combine that with the breakneck speed of 21st-century life and it's easy to lose our bearings and get lost.

Staying on Course with the Four Questions

The Four Questions provide perspective, vision, clarity, transparency, and direction. You may feel stuck. You may face a confusing array of options. You may feel as if things are moving too fast or you need an antidote against complacency. You may sometimes feel like life has been reduced to a series of birthdays. If so, ask yourself:

Who are you and what do you want?

Where are you and why are you there?

What will you do and how will you do it?

Who are your allies and how can they help?

Do your answers suggest that you need a change? Only you can determine that. Change is difficult for all of us. On the other hand, change for the sake of change can feel like whiplash. What's needed is productive change—change that's created by redesigning your future; change that allows you to get rid of excess baggage and travel light. Change that differentiates you without isolating you.

Only vending machines and babies like change.

One of the benefits of knowing who you are is that you will seldom be blindsided by whatever life throws at you. And in the face of a crisis, you will know that nothing harmful can touch you in a permanent way. You learn to learn from your failures. They put your values to the test.

"When we connect our plans to personal meaning, we develop the endurance to handle the tough times," says Catherine Kinney. "Clarity of what we want creates the standards that keep us moving forward when the wind is in our face." Clarity creates hope, and people with hope don't overreact to negativism or setbacks. When you are clear on where you are going, you don't overreact. You move past anxiety. Rather than being diffused by problems, your energy becomes focused like a laser. There is no problem that comes your way that's unsolvable.

As financier Warren Buffett says, "When the tide goes out, you discover who's been swimming naked." Living the Four Questions keep us clothed, even during the low tides of life.

What Is Your Legacy?

Too many people step on the stage of life and feel that they don't know their lines. They are confused, frustrated, frightened, or embarrassed. What a confidence-building feeling it is to know the plotline—to know where the story is going! That knowledge creates excitement, a sense of anticipation, and a feeling of assurance that produces exhilaration and even joy in the midst of change. We asked Coach John Wooden on his 96th birthday why at his age he was so enthusiastic and excited about life. He replied, "The moment your past becomes more exciting than your future is the day you start to die."

Understanding who you are and what you want creates harmony in your life. Without this it's like trying to connect with music when you are tone deaf. You can't tell whether you're in tune. So start with the goal of clarity. When you know who you are, what you want tends to follow. As Frances Hesselbein said, "Service to others and a passion for your own mission and work create a powerful synergy. It's about seeing how your strengths and passions align with the needs you see and are in a position to meet."

> "The moment your past becomes more exciting than your future is the day you start to die."
> —John Wooden

Working with PRIDE

Mike Ziegler is an individual who really understands that people can never be satisfied by more and more material things in their lives. Mike was the general manager of two large retail companies and owned another chain. He described himself as motivated and driven by making lots of money.

"There is nothing wrong with making lots of money," Mike said, "but somehow I realized that who I am is not what I have."

In the early 1980s, Mike retired from his retail businesses and moved to the foothills of Sacramento. He was prepared to enjoy family life and eventually plan his next career. He had no idea how quickly and dramatically his life was about to change. Shortly after his "retirement," he was invited to visit a local nonprofit organization, Placer Rehabilitation Industries, which had been started some years back in the basement of a church by a group of parents who had children with disabilities. The mission of PRI was to provide better lives and futures for these children.

Mike's untapped passion to do something bigger than himself was ignited, and he joined the company. Within two years, the non-profit company, now known as PRIDE, had more than quadrupled its revenues and number of employees. Today it has about four thousand employees and revenues well in excess of $100 million.

Working with and for people with disabilities changed Mike's life and his priorities, and he continues to reflect on doing things for a greater cause. "The longer I work at PRIDE, the more I know that none of us have a remote clue to what truly happens when somebody who couldn't get a job suddenly gets a job."

How Do You Define Success?

Aristotle noted that happiness is composed of many desired ends, not just one. People go mad seeking success, and many go even madder once they possess it.

Your personal journey for the best of your life has many possible destinations. Enjoy every trip, every new start, every detour, and every arrival. Enjoy all the people you meet; they are with you because they trust you and the direction you're going. After all, you are in command of your journey. You are the one who moves your life from good, to better, to best!

The Beginning of a Better Life

Many of the people with whom we have worked say that keeping a journal of their progress for the first three months of their journey was a small discipline that made the significant changes in their life more permanent and maintainable. Often it resulted in keeping a journal permanently because of the positive results. Those who do take the time to journal say that getting up 30 minutes earlier than usual is all that's needed. Start by getting up 5 minutes earlier, then 10, then 15, until after six weeks you wake up 30 minutes earlier without an alarm clock. Don't be surprised that if after a few months you are getting up an hour earlier and you are exercising and going for a walk as well. When you take control of how your day starts, you will maintain that positive feeling for longer and longer periods—until it lasts all day. What does the result of doing that look like? It looks like you are confident, engaged, personable, thoughtful, truthful, kind, and loving your life!

Have you found that the things that most concerned you or that you were afraid to come to grips with in the past seem diminished, neutralized, or gone altogether? If not, you may want to refer to some of the earlier chapters in the book and review. Even if you haven't decided today precisely what you will do to make improvements in your life, undoubtedly you are now keenly aware of what those changes need to be. In time the appropriate options, choices, and decisions will become clear when you respond to the Four Questions:

Who are you and what do you want? What are the cores of your personal strengths, passions, and aspirations? How will you erase the imagination gridlock that has kept you from going after your authentic goals?

Where are you and why are you there? You are now creating your own life map because you better understand how you have arrived where you are right now. You have just reviewed your past choices and decisions and recognize any faulty thoughts and belief systems that have gone undetected. And now you know the significance of the good choices and decisions you have made that bear repeating.

What will you do and how will you do it? It's great to dream, but whenever your dreams collide with reality, reality always wins. Now you have a fresh perspective to ensure a more successful, enjoyable career and personal life journey. In the days and months to come, you will become more and more calm and confident about what you will do and how you will do it.

Who are your allies and how can they help? Your stable relationships are key in accomplishing your life goals. Your relationships with your family, loved ones, friends, and coworkers will never be the same. You now know how to better preserve and protect those relationships, and you will get even better with time. Flying solo isn't fun or safe for long stretches of time, and you will never lack for friends or allies because now you are a better and trusted friend and ally as well.

Now that you are familiar with the Four Questions, you will find that your answers to the questions are far more meaningful to you.

You are now ready to take your own *Who Are You? What Do You Want?* Personal Retreat. Prepare to make it a special time for yourself—two nights and days to review and assess your life. You have decided to direct the only life over which you can ever have total control—your own. You are now about to enter a new chapter in your life. This is self-leadership in its finest form. Afterward you will return to home and work with renewed vigor, giving every day your all, enjoying being with the people you work with, appreciating those you love, having fun, and planning to encourage others around you to prepare for their own retreat.

Stay true to your path. You are now beginning the journey to the best of your life for the rest of your life!

EIGHT

Your 48-Hour Personal Retreat

What lies behind you and what lies before you are tiny matters when compared to what lies within you.

—Ralph Waldo Emerson

There is no better way to design a better future for yourself, your family, and your career than taking a day—preferably two—away from your usual routine to reflect on who you are and what you want.

Clients who have used our *Who Am I and What Do I Want?* Personal Retreat, either privately or in corporate retreat settings, tell us that they were surprised how the time they set aside to reflect on their lives affected them on a deep level and made it much easier for them to put their personal and work goals into action. Many make it an annual event to refresh and renew the length and breadth of their lives at home and work, and they say it helps them make adjustments to calibrate their lives. Continual renewal ensures long-lasting enjoyment of what will become the best years of your life!

This chapter serves as your catalyst for planning what is appropriate to you and the life you want to lead. What follows is an outline of exercises designed to help you think about your life using the Four Questions. Use these exercises to guide you through your own reflective journey. By the end of your retreat you won't have any hesitation in answering the question, "Who are you and what do you want?"

Preparation for the Retreat

Your personal retreat is exactly that—personal. It is important that you spend time alone. Urge others to support or encourage you, as you will them when they take their retreat.

No worthwhile retreat happens without preparation. Start by arranging to go somewhere special—a quiet place where you can stay alone for approximately 48 hours. It may be a mountain retreat; a tent in a quiet campsite; somewhere by the beach, lake, or desert; or just a favorite place where you are comfortable and won't be interrupted by television, cell phone, email, or PDA.

Plan ahead for hydration, healthy meals and snacks, hygiene, and medical necessities. Bring comfortable clothes and shoes appropriate to your chosen destination. Fresh air and a little activity will help stimulate your thinking. You may want to take walks in the woods or on the beach, hike in the mountains, or go swimming. Check the weather forecast to be prepared.

During your retreat, progress at your own pace. The exercises are designed to build on one another, leading you through a reflective personal journey. Write your thoughts, truths, concerns, ideas, desires, hopes, realities, and dreams in your Retreat Journal, or use your laptop and follow the formats suggested in each exercise. Or write your comments on the pages of this book to review in a few months. We also encourage you to record all your thoughts, insights, and epiphanies apart from the retreat exercises. Write whatever comes to mind; allow your imagination to venture far past its present boundaries. You will remember things from your life

Checklist for Your Perfect Retreat

You will find it useful to bring the following items for your personal retreat:

- ☐ Laptop computer
- ☐ Pens, pencils, pencil sharpener
- ☐ Notebook or journal
- ☐ Professional and personal calendars for the past 12 months
- ☐ Blank paper
- ☐ Your favorite music
- ☐ Small sheets of poster board
- ☐ Colored markers or pencils
- ☐ Photographs and memorabilia from significant events and different stages of your life
- ☐ Camera

you thought were long forgotten, and now they will take on a new meaning.

Beginning Your Retreat

Once you arrive at your quiet place, unpack and settle into your workspace. Breathe in deeply and exhale slowly a few times until you are feeling relaxed. Take a picture of yourself before you begin. Now take a few pictures of the setting you have chosen, indoors and out. Your photos can serve as a reminder of your retreat during the months and years that follow. Preview the exercises that follow. The questions are straightforward, designed to build on one another, but if you don't have an answer right away, feel free to put a question or two aside and return to them later. Or review the section of the book or your "For Reflection" notes to which the question refers. You are in complete control of your retreat!

Before you go to Exercise 1, answer the following questions.

What do I value?

What is important to me? What do I value most in my life?

What Do I Believe?

What do I believe? Write a series of one-sentence belief statements; for example, "I believe in forgiveness."

Exercise 1: My Roles and Relationships

My Role

List below or on a piece of paper all the roles you currently play in life (for example, parent, sibling, son/daughter, boss, housekeeper, gardener, chauffeur, personal event planner, financial investor, role model, babysitter, nurse, confidant, psychologist, neighbor, friend, grandparent, aunt/uncle). Your answers will help take you to the core of who you are—your personal talents, passions, and obligations.

_____

_____

_____

_____

_____

_____

_____

_____

_____

_____

_____

_____

_____

_____

_____

From the list you have created, select four roles that are the most important to you at this stage of your life.

1. _____

2. _____

3. _____

4. _____

For each of the roles you've selected, respond to the statements "What I believe others expect of me in this role" and "What I expect of myself in this role." See the following example, which involves the role of parent, and use the four pages that follow or your Retreat Journal to record your own comments.

Your Role: Example

Role: Parent

What I believe others expect of me regarding this role	What I expect of myself regarding this role
provide emotional support for my children	understand my children's needs; take time to understand my children's talents and potential
face any conflict with my kids, teachers, or school ASAP	help my kids develop their interests even though they may be nothing like mine
create a wholesome and enjoyable environment in our home	share concerns and discuss family decisions with my spouse and agree to present a united front with our children
take care of my children's health care and education	never criticize them publicly
attend their sports, recitals, and school events	plan time with kids on weekends and vacations during school breaks
make birthdays and holidays a priority	listen, really listen
pay our bills	

Role #1: _____

What I believe others expect of me regarding this role	What I expect of myself regarding this role

Role #2: _____

What I believe others expect of me regarding this role	What I expect of myself regarding this role

Role #3: _____

| What I believe others expect of me regarding this role | What I expect of myself regarding this role |

Role #4: _____

What I believe others expect of me regarding this role	What I expect of myself regarding this role

My Relationships

The Interdependence Model described and diagrammed on the following pages will help you examine the types of relationships you have right now. Two forces in your life are characterized by "togetherness" and "separateness." These forces stand in dynamic tension, pulling you in one direction or the other. Interdependence is an acquired balance between the two. It's something you learn to do; it rarely comes naturally.

Refer back to the four roles you described. Write the name of the person with whom you primarily relate in each role. Do you have a sense of interdependence with that person?

Once you see on paper your own relationship formulas—the patterns of how you interact with others—you can make better choices about your time, energy, and sense of engagement. Choosing a balanced life means your relationships with others are more enjoyable because you are more enthusiastically engaged. You are a magnet for other balanced people.

Altering any relationship takes thinking, patience, time, and focus. How might you better develop interdependence in all your relationships? Interdependence in any relationship begins with you. If you behave interdependently, you become the model for others close to you to follow. If you take the lead, the dance begins.

The Interdependence Model

To measure the dynamics of separateness and togetherness at work in each relationship, rate your agreement or disagreement with the following statements on a scale of 1 to 5 (1 means you strongly disagree; 5 means you strongly agree):

I don't really care about what others think.   ☐

I seldom ask others for help.   ☐

My preference is to work alone.   ☐

Total Independent   ☐

I value other people's opinions more than my own.   ☐

When others get angry with me, I blame myself.   ☐

I find it difficult to stand up for myself.   ☐

Total Dependent   ☐

I find myself being oversensitive to other people's needs.   ☐

I feel better about myself when people need me.   ☐

I function better when someone is dependent on me.   ☐

Total Codependent   ☐

I think it is important for the people in my life
to have their own space.   ☐

I am able to share my opinion with others
without fear of losing the relationship.   ☐

If I take someone's advice, I don't blame
that person if it doesn't work out.   ☐

Total Interdependent   ☐

Place each total in the appropriate box in the Interdependence Model grid that follows.

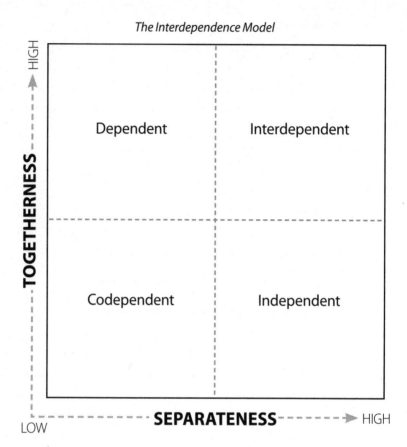

The Interdependence Model

What do your scores mean? Separateness measures your need for autonomy. Togetherness measures your need for connectivity. If you scored from 1 to 5 in any of the categories, it is not your primary way of interacting in a relationship. If you scored from 6 to 10 in any category, it may be your secondary way of interacting. If you scored from 11 to 15 in any category, it is likely your primary way of interacting in a relationship.

Interdependence Model Definitions

The following descriptions explain how you relate to others.

Dependent: In this kind of relationship you constantly defer to others to make decisions for you. Your identity is tied to the way others feel about and react to you. What people say or don't say to you or about you can make or break your day. The danger in this is that your life is slowly and often imperceptibly taken over by others.

Independent: You prefer acting alone. You may appear to be inattentive to others and at worst self-absorbed, when that may not be your intention. The danger is that you isolate yourself from others, making intimate relationships more difficult.

Codependent: Your sense of self is defined by your relationship with others. There are no boundaries between your true self and others. It is difficult for you to say no. You put yourself last. You also attempt to control others by taking responsibility for them. You often find yourself in tightly tangled relationships.

Interdependent: In this model there is a healthy balance between yourself and others. You are able to differentiate where you end and others begin. You take responsibility and ownership for your own actions and at the same time are influenced and affected by others. You recognize your need to interact with others without depending on their changing moods to shape who you are.

For Reflection

When you identify the roles you play and the relationships that are critical to those roles, you can then move on to examining those roles and relationships more closely. The following questions will help you understand not only the roles that you see for yourself but how they are played out in the context of your relationships.

1. Are you controlling or being controlled?

2. Do you have a healthy balance between receiving and giving in your relationships?

3. In what ways would you like to maintain or change how you relate to others?

4. What relationships are most precious to you?

5. How would you like those relationships to look in the future?

Exercise 2: Your Lifeline

Imagine a path that stretches from the beginning of your life to where you are today. We call that a lifeline, and in this exercise you will illustrate your lifeline.

Your lifeline can help you review your past—where you came from—and determine where you are now. Have you taken yourself for granted in the past? How does your life now compare to the life you had growing up? It is critical to see where you have come from to do a better job planning your future.

Take a large piece of paper or poster board on which to draw your path. Your line can look like a road, a path through the woods, a shoreline, a sidewalk, or a simple line. It can be as plain or creative or crazy as you like. As you draw your lifeline, fill in significant details of your life so far. At the start write your birth date and at the end today's date. Along the path list every significant event, celebration, birth, death, disappointment, education and career advancement, relationship, accomplishment, time of hardship, sadness, or peak experience. Mark the times you laughed most, the times you were so happy you cried or broke out into song, and the times your tears came from sorrow. Use marking pens, crayons, ink, or pastels—anything that will make it fun for you.

Don't worry about your artistic ability; just let yourself go. As you work you'll remember events, significant relationships, and what happened with them. Write every event as it occurs to you, big or small.

Here are some questions to help you put together your lifeline. If possible, write the date of each event or episode.

What were the peak experiences in your life—the ones filled with emotion, such as your graduation, your wedding, or your first child graduating from high school? Spend some time reliving those experiences. When did they happen? How did you feel? Did you laugh? Did you celebrate? Visualize the experiences from beginning to end. What was it about each experience that made it significant for you? Make a list of all the strengths, skills, talents, abilities, and resources you used in your peak experiences. Who was with you? Where were you?

Here are some other questions to help you move this exercise:

What were the most emotional times in your life?

What made the difference between feeling down or feeling great?

What were you most interested in while growing up?

Who were the people who had the most influence in your life?

What were some of your major decisions?

What were the highlights in elementary school, middle school, high school, and college? What were the lowlights?

What were some of the biggest changes that happened to you?

When were you most successful?

When did you feel like a failure?

Whom did you love?

And who loved you?

What were your most significant work experiences?

What were your most significant family experiences?

With whom are your most important friendships? Why are they particularly important to you?

Whom do you admire most at work?

Who are the most important people in your life? Why?

Exercise 3: Measuring My Strengths

Many people are unable to articulate their strengths but find it easy to list their faults and weaknesses. If you have the same tendency, try to think of how you can turn that perceived weakness into a strength. For example, if you feel that you take too long to make a decision, that quality can become a strength when you think about your caution and term it *thoughtful* or *deliberate*. Look for the lighter side of each of your qualities and use the two lists you create below in your self-analysis that follows.

My strengths are	Areas in which I need to improve are

Make a note to call or email a close friend or family member once you return home and ask them what they see as your strengths as well as areas you need to improve. Are these answers different from what you recorded during your retreat? If so, why do you suppose that is? If these responses echo what you have said, you have already learned or have begun to learn to see yourself as others see you.

Self-Analysis

What do I perceive that other people think are my strengths?

What do I believe that other people think are my weaknesses?

What are the obstacles that get in the way of my being successful?

Is there anything that is difficult for me to admit about myself?

What are the top three areas in which I would like to improve?

Exercise 4: Four Dimensions of Myself

Fill in the "Discovering Who I Am" grid (refer to Chapter 6 for a description of the four quadrants of our model based on the Johari Window). Think carefully about your answers. Be truthful with yourself.

Discovering Who I Am

Open and Authentic What I know about myself and allow others to know about me (e.g., I am generous)	**Blind Spots** What others see in me but I don't or can't see about myself (e.g., what do you think others say your blind spots are?)
The Secret Self What I know about myself that others don't know about me (e.g., I struggle with anxiety)	**Unknown Potential** What others don't see in me and I don't yet know about myself (e.g., what type of adventures or activities could help reveal who you are?)

Exercise 5: Inner Dialogue

Self-Talk

Self-talk is the dialogue that goes on inside your head when you are faced with conflict, life challenges, or even simple day-to-day concerns. The previous exercise gives you a more accurate perception of who you are and what others believe you are. Your belief about who you are influences your self-talk. This aspect of your mind engages in a running commentary about everything you do. It never lets anything go by without some comment, remark, or evaluation. Although self-talk can be both good and bad, it is the negative self-talk that sabotages us. In the following lists, you may recognize some of the negative thoughts because you may have heard them all your life. These thoughts are usually formed during childhood from comments you heard from a parent, teacher, or someone in authority. Now as an adult you have incorporated them into your own personality. You don't need those people to tell you what to do anymore. It's about time to cut them loose, and you'll learn how to in the next two exercises.

But you can turn almost any negative to the positive if you are self-aware. Read the following list and then go through the exercise with your own thoughts.

Negative Self-Talk	Positive Self-Talk
I'm not smart enough.	I'm smart enough.
Something is wrong.	A lot about my life is right.
I can't do it.	I can do it.

Negative Self-Talk	Positive Self-Talk
I have to do everything around here or it won't get done.	I am relaxed and letting go.
What are they thinking about me?	Everything is easy once you do it.
I can never be on time.	Change takes time, and I am patient and disciplined.
I'm not organized.	People love and appreciate me the way I want them to.
I'm not the weight I want to be.	I enjoy getting worthwhile things done by doing them right the first time.
I never finish anything.	It doesn't matter what people think about me as long as I know that I am honest with myself.
This is too hard.	I live my values.
Change takes too long.	
People will never love and appreciate me the way I want them to.	

Your Self-Talk: Before and After

In the left-hand column, record your negative self-talk dialogue. What do you say to yourself throughout the day? Then transform the negative self-talk you wrote in the left-hand column and transform your words into positive, self-motivating, and self-inspiring self-talk. Think about the positive truths you've just written and about how you will incorporate your new self-talk into your life.

Negative Self-Talk | **Positive Self-Talk**

Now would be a good time to take a walk and think about how much stronger you feel. Take in some deep breaths and pick up your pace. If you are walking and other people are around you, observe them and ask yourself what kind of self-talk those strangers are saying to themselves. Is it negative or is it positive? How can you tell? Is it becoming more obvious to you? Later when you get back to your book, journal, or computer, record your observations.

Exercise 6: My Experiences

Describe the greatest successes in your life. (You may want to refer back to your lifeline.)

What new information did you learn, and how were you affected by your success?

Describe your greatest failures. What were the lessons learned?

What were your most significant work experiences?

What have been the most significant decisions in your life?

What do you enjoy today as a result of those decisions?

Did you get the results you wanted? What were the immediate results? What were the long-term results? How is your life better (or worse) today as a result of making those decisions?

Would you do anything differently? What lessons did you learn?

What would you repeat in a similar situation?

Exercise 7: My Preferred Self

Life Dreams

Make a list of your dreams for your life. Look as far into the future as you like and include work, family, social, and personal. Beside each dream, list the realities that will help you fulfill the dream and those that may limit it. Be specific about how these realities may favor or limit your dreams.

Below is a list of a few areas you may want to focus on during this exercise. You may pick more than one category or invent others.

Health
Lifestyle
Career
Relationships
Spirituality
Education
Home
Work
Travel/Vacation

For each dream in each category, write down where you are. For example:

Health: *My cholesterol level is 212.*

Lifestyle: *I am living in a foreign country and I don't speak the language.*

Career: *I have been giving my job only a percentage of what I am capable of, and that is interfering with my success.*

Relationships: *My most personal relationship is not what it once was.*

Spirituality: *My beliefs and my behavior do not match.*

Education: *Others who have the kind of job I want have an MBA.*

For each category, write down where you want to be. Get used to saying, "I want . . ." For example:

Health: *I want my cholesterol level to be under 200.*

Lifestyle: *I want to speak conversational German in six months.*

Career: *I want to be promoted in one year.*

Relationships: *I want to make my most personal relationship meaningful, intimate, exciting, and full of laughter.*

Spirituality: *I want to feel congruent and feel that no matter where I am, I am myself.*

Education: *I want to apply to the schools that I want to have on my résumé.*

For each category you choose, write down action steps that you believe are necessary to achieve your desired result. For example:

Health: *Walk on treadmill at office fitness center for 30 minutes three times a week.*

Lifestyle: *Purchase German language course; listen during morning drive.*

Career: *Review my performance reviews for past three years. Study position requirements for next level.*

Relationships: *Schedule an evening out with my spouse.*

Spirituality: *Schedule 10 minutes of quiet reflection at home each weekday morning.*

Education: *Check the websites of the schools; bookmark the application pages; complete one application a week.*

My Life Dream for Health

Where I am:

Where I want to be:

Action steps:

My Life Dream for Lifestyle

Where I am:

Where I want to be:

Action steps:

My Life Dream for Career

Where I am:

Where I want to be:

Action steps:

My Life Dream for Relationships

Where I am:

Where I want to be:

Action steps:

My Life Dream for Spirituality

Where I am:

Where I want to be:

Action steps:

My Life Dream for Education

Where I am:

Where I want to be:

Action steps:

My Life Dream for

Where I am:

Where I want to be:

Action steps:

A Practically Perfect Day

Nothing is ever perfect, but describe a near-perfect day for you five years from today: Where are you? Take a mental snapshot. How have you incorporated your dreams (what you wrote about in the previous section) into that day? In your perfect day, who is with you? What are you doing? How do you feel? What expression is on your face? Are you worried? Smiling? Does your body feel relaxed?

_____

_____

_____

_____

_____

_____

_____

_____

_____

_____

Exercise 8: Professional and Personal Change

Forces of Change

In Chapter 5 we presented a simple model for making change called Force Field Analysis. On one side of the situation are forces that help you carry out change, and on the other side are forces that hinder change. It is important to identify both the forces that help you change and the forces that work against changing your professional and personal life for the better. The key is to choose the forces for change and withdraw your support from those opposed to change.

Use the following information and the chart on the following page as models to create several changes for your life, one for each. Identify each change or improvement about yourself that you want to make. Then identify the forces restraining you from achieving your preferred future and the forces encouraging the change.

Force Field Analysis

Write the desired change in your life (your preferred future) in the center of the chart ("The Change Issue"). You can repeat this exercise for any number of changes that you wish to make.

Record what forces restrain you from achieving your preferred future. List them on the right side of the diagram. On a scale of 1 to 5, label their strength. (1 is the weakest; 5 is the strongest.)

Write down the forces that encourage change. List them on the left side of the diagram. On a scale of 1 to 5, label their strength. (1 is the weakest; 5 is the strongest.)

Which of your strengths can you draw on to weaken the restraining forces and strengthen the forces for change?

What additional support or advice do you need to reach your preferred future? How and when will you get that advice? Later, how will you show those who support you and/or give you advice that you appreciate the help they give you?

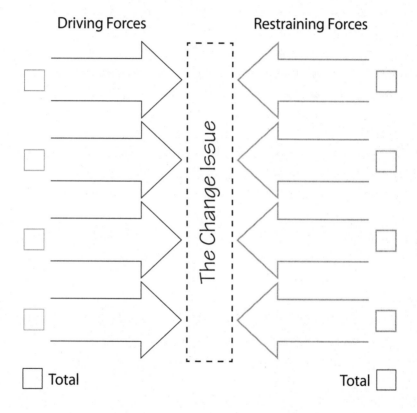

Driving Forces

Restraining Forces

The Change Issue

Total

Total

Exercise 9: My Goals

Set SMART Goals
Specific, Measurable, Attainable, Relevant, Time-bound

This exercise is a crucial part of your life improvement process. You may want to refer to Chapter 5 to review SMART goals. Although you may have set business and personal goals in the past, this time you can do it with more clarity and purpose by answering the following questions, which focus on the resources, actions, and measure of success for each of your goals. Then write down your goals. Setting priorities for your goals is very important. Select three to five goals that are most critical for your personal and your business or work goals. Notice the difference with which you approach articulating your goals after a little self-intervention and reflection:

_____

_____

_____

_____

Which aspects of your life would you like to improve? (You may wish to refer to your answers from Exercise 8.)

_____

_____

_____

_____

How will you keep track of your progress? What are the best and easiest ways you can demonstrate your improvement to yourself? What simple monitoring system can you use?

_____

_____

_____

_____

How can you clarify your targets or goals and make them meaningful? What's at stake? What deadline are you shooting for?

_____

_____

_____

_____

Who needs to know and who cares most about your progress? Are there others who can help you? What kind of feedback will be most helpful to you: your own, others', or a combination?

_____

_____

_____

_____

How are you going to maintain your improvements? How can you set up a personal means of recognition to gauge your progress? How will you benchmark and celebrate your successes?

_____

_____

_____

_____

How can you evaluate what you accomplished? To what kind of standards do you hold yourself? Once you have succeeded, will you want to establish new goals?

_____

_____

_____

_____

Feedback

Feedback should be immediate, objective, specific, and directly related to your goals and targets. It should be simple, understandable, and given on a regular basis. Effective feedback is also descriptive rather than evaluative, and never mean-spirited, critical, or sarcastic. Feedback is a helpful way of giving and receiving help, especially if you want to learn how to match your behavior with your intentions.

Give yourself feedback by considering some or all of the following, first with respect to your work, then your home life:

1. Review what you did this week.

2. How does it compare with your previous week?

3. Set three priorities for next week.

4. Will you want help with what you want to achieve?

5. If you'd like assistance or advice, how might you ask for it in a way that a busy person will want to help you? Later, how will you say thanks?

6. Think about ways to improve your behavior, thinking, habits, and favorite hobbies or sport activities.

7. What have you read or observed recently that has made an impact?

8. What have been your recent accomplishments?

9. What progress have you made in your habits, skills, and relationships?

10. Write next week's action plan.

Marty's SMART Goals

Marty is a good manager in an organization in northern California. In a performance review he was told by business colleagues that they did not perceive him to be a good listener. His wife, Janet, agreed with that assessment. Marty asked for help and set up a SMART goal plan. He started by asking himself why he did not listen carefully to others. He wrote the following:

I hear very little because I'm thinking about what I think the other person is really thinking or feeling.

I am thinking about what I am going to say next.

I change the topic very quickly and focus on myself.

It's like I have a filter in my brain: I hear only what I want to hear.

I hear what the other person said, but I quickly discount it.

I start to think about something else. I get bored easily.

Marty's SMART goals:

Specific: Improve my listening skills first with my wife, Janet.

Measurable: I will ask Janet after each time we interact, "On a scale from 1 to 5—1 is poor, 5 is great—what is your perception of me as a listener?" I will carry a piece of paper and mark down Janet's rating. Is it different from the rating I gave myself? If so, why? Gather some ratings during the first week to serve as a baseline. Am I the same Monday through Friday as I am on the weekend?

Attainable: I was averaging a 2 from her feedback during the first week, so I set a goal to get to be a 4 within a month's time.

Relevant: This is an important skill that will improve our marriage, especially as our children reach their teenage years and we need to work together as parents.

Time-bound: Set weekly improvement targets; see overall improvement within one month.

Marty realized that altering a few key behaviors, such as increasing eye contact, staying on the topic, and asking relevant questions, made a major difference in his wife's perception of his listening. Within two weeks he rated between a 3 and 4 on his personal measurement chart, up from his starting point of 2. And by listening to her, he demonstrated to her how important she is to him.

Marty also developed his listening skills by asking his colleagues and friends to give him honest feedback. He told his closest friends what he was doing with Janet and asked them to remind him if he seemed not to be listening to her or to them. That step showed Janet how important the goal had become to Marty.

My SMART Goal

Use the following prompts and questions to create your own SMART goal plan.

Specific:

_____

_____

_____

_____

_____

_____

Measurable:

_____

_____

_____

_____

_____

_____

Attainable:

_____

_____

_____

_____

_____

_____

Relevant:

_____

_____

_____

_____

_____

_____

Time-bound:

_____

_____

_____

_____

_____

Resources

What resources must I allocate?

How much time must I give to this goal?

Will there need to be changes in my schedule?

Who can help me?

Action

What will I do in the next 6 to 12 months?

What will I do in the next 1 to 5 years?

What have others done to achieve this goal?

What resistance must be minimized for this goal to be achieved?

Measures of Success

How will I measure my success with regard to this goal?

How will I celebrate my progress toward my goal?

Who are my allies and how can they help?

Exercise 10: My Allies

Mentors

People who grow—professionally, personally, and spiritually—share something in common: they are involved in mentoring relationships. If you look back on your past, you will recall people who have been your mentors. Now may be a good time to take out your photo or school albums and think about people who have in some way influenced who you are today. In your journal write the names of people you believe have helped shape your life and how they've helped you. Following is a summary of the types of mentors you may have had. (See also Chapter 6.)

Upward Mentors: People who have helped you become who you are—a grandparent, parent, coach, author, or someone you have never met personally.

Friendship Mentors: People with whom you have experienced the stages of life—college, career, family, and so on.

Sandpaper Mentors: People who have rubbed you the wrong way in life but have helped sharpen you.

Downward Mentors: People in whom you have invested your time, energy, and thoughts.

Having reflected on the relationships that were important in shaping who you are today, now think about the people who can help you shape the life you desire. Write down the names of people you believe are important to your personal and career development now.

For each person you mentioned, write the type of mentor he or she is to you and the role each may play in helping you in implementing your goals. Consider each person in light of the following questions:

> Why is this person a good and reliable mentor? How long have I known this person? Do I trust him or her as my ally?

> How can this person assist or advise me in realizing my desired future?

> How can I use what I have learned to help others as others have helped me?

Choose two people from your mentor list and write them a letter sharing with them the ways they have helped shape your life.

Be a Mentor

To whom might you be a mentor in the future? How?

_____

_____

_____

_____

_____

_____

Exercise 11: Appreciating What You Have

More Good Thoughts

Consider the good things happening in your life right now. Write your thoughts in your journal, using the following questions to help prompt your reflection.

What do you enjoy most about the life you have created so far?

How do you continue or duplicate those kinds of experiences?

Who are your loved ones? How do you reciprocate what they do for you?

How do your friends, family, and associates know you appreciate them?

What attention do you offer others in terms of time, consideration, and enjoyment?

Are you early or on time for your appointments with others?

Do you give others your undivided attention?

Do you really listen to others, or are you thinking about what you are going to say before they finish? Do you look into their eyes when you speak with them?

After your personal retreat has ended, how will you make your interactions with everyone you encounter more significant, pleasant, and enjoyable?

Exercise 12: The Big Picture

Memories Made and Memories in the Making

Look at the most recent photographs you have with you. What feelings come up as you look at them: gratitude, appreciation, comfort, or something else? Write those feelings or reactions on a separate page or in your journal.

Think about ways you will create new, positive experiences in the year ahead—experiences that, when you review them during future retreats, you will remember with strong, positive feelings. Describe those experiences. Where are you? What are you doing? Who is with you?

As one of your action steps toward achieving your personal success plan, set a date on your calendar to revisit the work you have done on your personal retreat (preferably one year from now).

Now is a good time to take another picture of yourself. How does it compare with the picture you took before your retreat started? (The beauty of digital or cell phone cameras is that they give you instant feedback. And you can add your photo to your electronic journal, if you are keeping one.) If someone you love and who loves you were to look at your picture, how might he or she describe you? Write your answer in your journal and refer to it often in the months to come.

It's now time to congratulate yourself for doing something that will forevermore alter the way you look at your life, your work, and the people with whom you surround yourself. Think now, how different life might be if people all over the world would take two days to reflect and think about the best way to continue their lives.

In the end, the only things we have control over are our beliefs, our attitude, and how we choose to live our lives. By making better choices about small matters and better decisions about important matters, we master the kind of self-leadership that Ken Blanchard talked about in the foreword. Now it's your turn to lead yourself, and by doing so, through example, you will lead others to do the same.

We invite you to share your own stories of your retreat and how it affected you at work and home at our website, www.whoareyou book.com. Meanwhile, enjoy every step of your journey.

NOTES

Chapter 1

1. J. Gosling and H. Mintzberg, "Five Minds of a Manager," *Harvard Business Review* (November 2003).

2. Michael J. Silverstein and Neil Fiske, *Trading Up: Why Consumers Want New Luxury Goods—And How Companies Create Them* (New York: Portfolio/Penguin Group USA, 2003).

3. Gregg Easterbrook, *The Progress Paradox* (New York: Random House, 2004); "The Search for Meaning," *Trends Magazine* (July 2004), www.trends-magazine.com/trend.php/Trend/1009/Category/56.

Chapter 3

1. George Reavis, *The Animal School* (Peterborough, NH: Crystal Springs Books, 1999).

Chapter 4

1. Center for Creative Leadership, www.ccl.org/leadership/pdf/news/newsletters/acrosstheboard.pdf and www.ccl.org/leadership/update/2004/AUGtransition.aspx?pageId=966.

Chapter 5

1. Kurt Lewin, "Defining the Field at a Given Time," *Psychological Review* 50 (1943): 292–310.

2. J. C. Norcross, A. C. Ratzin, and D. Payne, "Ringing in the New Year: The Change Processes and Reported Outcomes of Resolutions," *Addictive Behaviors* 14 (1989): 205–212.

Chapter 6

1. J. Robert Clinton and Paul D. Stanley, *Connecting: The Mentoring Relationships You Need to Succeed in Life* (Colorado Springs, CO: NavPress, 1992).

2. J. Luft and H. Ingham, "The Johari Window: A Graphic Model of Interpersonal Awareness," *Proceedings of the Western Training Laboratory in Group Development* (Los Angeles: UCLA, 1955).

SERVICES AND RESOURCES

Mick Ukleja frequently gives keynote speeches on the subjects of Managing the Next Generation, Teamwork, Transformational Leadership, The Power of Empowerment, Ethical Leadership, Who Are You and What Do You Want? and many more.

To learn more about Mick and LeadershipTraQ, please visit:

www.whoareyoubook.com

www.leadershiptraq.com

www.genextconsulting.com

www.ucel.org

Bob Lorber is a personal coach for CEOs and business leaders throughout the world. He is a highly regarded management consultant who works with executive teams to improve their leadership skills, personal effectiveness, and the overall performance of their companies.

Bob offers consulting services, executive coaching, and executive retreats. He gives keynote speeches on the subjects of Leadership and Change, Doing What Matters, Productivity Improvement, Team Development and Personal Life Planning, and Who Are You and What Do You Want? Bob and his organization help align learning and improvement needs with business and individual strategies for long-term impact.

To learn more, visit www.whoareyoubook.com.

To learn more about Lorber Kamai Consulting, visit:

www.lorberkamai.com

www.levylorber.com

APPRECIATION AND PRAISE

We would like to thank our agent and partner, Margret McBride, for her extraordinary support of *Who Are You? What Do You Want?* She really made it happen. Her passion, talent, and involvement at every level helped make it fun and exciting, and she added the quality that makes this book something we are all very proud of. Margret brought out the best in all of us in thinking and writing, and in gathering the real-life examples that make this work come to life. We also want to thank her tireless team of Faye Atchison, Donna DeGutis, and Anne Bomke, who gave their all and were always there for us. Thank you, McBride Literary Agency. We will forever be grateful.

Thanks to:

Ken Blanchard for his continued support, friendship, and inspiration throughout our lives.

John Duff, publisher of Perigee Books at Penguin Group, for championing our book.

Jeanette Shaw, Amy Schneider, Jennifer Eck, Charles Bjorklund, and Tiffany Estreicher for their involvement in the publishing process.

Chip Espinoza for his ideas and insights on the personal retreat.

Jim Dowd and his agency for making sure the right people get this life-changing message.

ABOUT THE AUTHORS

Mick Ukleja is the founder and president of LeadershipTraQ, a leadership-consulting firm based in California. He hosts *LeadershipTraQ Televised*, an interview-format talk show in Southern California that profiles outstanding leaders. He helped found the Ukleja Center for Ethical Leadership at California State University, Long Beach, the second-largest university in the state. He has worked with entrepreneurs and corporate executives of businesses and organizations ranging from Boeing to the Special Olympics. Mick also serves as chairman of the Board of Trustees for the Astronauts Memorial Foundation at the Kennedy Space Center, which oversees the Center for Space Education. He is a principal in the Bonita Bay Group, one of the largest developers of master-planned communities in southwest Florida. Dr. Ukleja holds a bachelor's degree in philosophy, a master's degree in Semitic languages, and a PhD in theology.

Robert Lorber is president of the Lorber Kamai Consulting Group, formed in Orange County, California. The organization has developed and implemented productivity improvement systems for companies on five continents. Its client roster includes Kraft Foods, Teichert Inc., Occidental Petroleum, Gillette, American Express, Mattel, AlliedSignal, Raley's, VSP, Wells Fargo, Pillsbury, Pfizer, and many other medium-sized and Fortune 500 companies. Robert is an internationally recognized expert and published author on executive coaching, performance management, teamwork, and strategy development. He is the coauthor with Ken Blanchard of the *New York Times* and international bestseller *Putting the One Minute Manager to Work*. He coauthored *Safety 24/7* with Gregory Anderson and *Doing What Matters* with Jim Kilts, former CEO of Gillette, and John Manfredi. Dr. Lorber received a master's degree in sociology and a PhD in organizational psychology.